... accompanied here – by virtue of a surrealist experiment in the bookbinder's craft – by AWFUL MOMENTS ... a selection of the dire and dreadful embarrassments suffered by the great and famous of the world. You'll learn what happened when George Brown invited the Bishop of Montevideo to dance to the National Anthem and when the groupie pushed Mick Jagger into a Black Forest gateau. You'll cringe with the tale of Brendan Behan and the Moss Bros dinner jacket and the story of the wife who took revenge on an unfaithful spouse with mustard and cress. Your toes will curl at what the Pope said to Princess Diana and what President Reagan says nearly all the time. Don't miss the guest appearances by such masters of the awful moment as John Gielgud, Sam Goldwyn and Harold Wilson – not to mention the Indian subcontinent and the more advanced practitioners of the Royal House of Windsor. Philip Norman himself makes more than one appearance amongst the Moments ... not infrequently in the role of victim.

Think of this volume as a sandwich. Between two thick slices of hilarity and merriment, you'll discover the filling – PIECES OF HATE ... a collection of sincere and deeply felt expressions of finely-honed nastiness, invective and abuse from a firing line of celebrated slanderers.

The most poisonous sandwich filling since those famous buffet parties at the Borgias' place ...

A modest exercise in manual dexterity will reveal that AWFUL MOMENTS is ...

D1369177

BY THE SAME AUTHOR

Novels

Slip On A Fat Lady
Plumridge
The Skaters' Waltz
Wild Thing (short stories)

Biography and Journalism

Shout: The True Story of the Beatles
The Stones
The Road Goes On For Ever
Tilt the Hourglass and Begin Again

Plays

The Man That Got Away
Skiffle

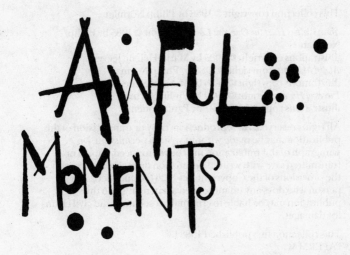

AWFUL MOMENTS

PHILIP NORMAN

Illustrated by Marie-Hélène Jeeves

PAPERMAC

This collection copyright © 1988 by Philip Norman

Your Walrus Hurt the One You Love copyright © 1985 by Philip Norman
illustrations copyright © 1985 by Marie-Hélène Jeeves
Awful Moments copyright © 1986 by Philip Norman
illustrations copyright © 1986 by Marie-Hélène Jeeves
Pieces of Hate copyright © 1987 by Philip Norman
illustrations copyright © 1987 by Paula Youens

All rights reserved. No reproduction, copy or transmission of this publication may be made without written permission. No paragraph of this publication may be reproduced, copied or transmitted save with written permission or in accordance with the provisions of the Copyright Act 1956 (as amended). Any person who does any unauthorised act in relation to this publication may be liable to criminal prosecution and civil claims for damages.

This collection first published 1988 by
PAPERMAC
a division of Macmillan Publishers Limited
4 Little Essex Street London WC2R 3LF
and Basingstoke

Associated companies in Auckland, Delhi, Dublin, Gaborone, Hamburg, Harare, Hong Kong, Johannesburg, Kuala Lumpur, Lagos, Manzini, Melbourne, Mexico City, Nairobi, New York, Singapore and Tokyo

British Library Cataloguing in Publication Data
Norman, Philip
The Norman trilogy
I. Title II. Norman, Philip. Your walrus hurt the one you love.
Norman Philip. Awful moments. Norman, Philip. Pieces of hate.
828'.91402'08

ISBN: 0-333-47447-X

Printed in Hong Kong

Your Walrus Hurt the One You Love, Awful Moments and *Pieces of Hate* were first published as separate volumes by Elm Tree Books, London, in 1985, 1986 and 1987 respectively.
Cover design by Marie-Hélène Jeeves

CONTENTS

CONTENTS

INTRODUCTION

'Oh yes, I know what you mean,' several friends said when canvassed for entries to this book. 'You want Embarrassing Moments. The sort that people used to tell to Wilfred Pickles. "'Ee, Wilfred — was my face scarlet, standing there with my drawers down round my ankles . . ."'

Let's get something straight. I don't just mean Embarrassing Moments. I mean Awful Moments. I mean moments which, recollected at howsoever great a remove of time, cause the stomach to lurch, the toes to cringe, the sphincter to shrivel, the sleeper to sit bolt upright in bed, sweating and exclaiming 'All right — what *else* could I have done?'

Friends, colleagues and readers of my pieces in *The Times* and *Sunday Times* have valiantly obliged. Mostly, though, I have delved back among stories told to me — and, inevitably, by me — during 25 years as a gossiping journalist. I have been blessed (maybe it's cursed) with a mind which retains anecdotes the way that red shiny material picks up fluff. This has been a highly enjoyable way of clearing out my mental lumber room.

Philosophical questions will, I fear, remain unanswered. For instance, is it worse to cause a truly awful moment or be witness to one? Man is unique among Earth's

1

species in sweating on behalf of his fellow creatures — a duty for which both Ronald Reagan's and Margaret Thatcher's ministers receive too little credit. I have touched but glancingly, too, on such questions of subtle and near-unfathomable awfulness as the things mothers come out with in company.

The stories are true, so far as I have been able to ascertain. Those I cannot personally vouch for seem too brimful of human lunacy to be otherwise. Occasionally, names have been left out to protect the guilty.

Lest I be accused of profiting from human misery, let me hasten to say that no one possesses the ingredients for awful moments in greater measure than myself. It has been but slowly revealed to me in adult life that tactlessness, ignorance, misjudgment, inopportune high spirits and a hopeless head for drink are not a personal monopoly. Just a moment ago, I rang a friend on *The Guardian* to discuss vague plans for lunch. 'What are you doing there now?' I asked him.

'Oh,' he replied lightly, 'they call me deputy editor.'

Philip Norman
London 1986

One of George Brown's drunker moments as Foreign Secretary found him staggering into a State gala in Rio more than an hour after it had officially begun.

The best way of absorbing himself into the assembly and evading the rigours of diplomatic conversation, he woozily decided, would be to get straight on to the dance floor. Lurching up to a vision in dark red, he mumbled 'Would you care to dance, Madam?'

'I will not dance with you,' the vision in dark red replied, 'for three reasons. Firstly you are drunk. Secondly, the band is playing the National Anthem. And thirdly I am the Bishop of Montevideo.'

✿

At the 1977 Commonwealth Prime Ministers' Conference, India was represented by Morarji Desai, the disciple of the Mahatma whose Janata party had briefly overthrown Indira Gandhi's rule.

It was known that Mr Desai was a strict vegetarian and, at the luncheon that inaugurated the Conference, special bowls of nuts and dried fruit were set out on the table for him.

During the pre-luncheon pleasantries, Audrey Callaghan, wife of the then Prime Minister, was standing near Mr Desai's vegan lunch. Mistaking the bowls for cocktail snacks, she emptied them.

✿

Shortly before General de Gaulle stepped down from power, he and his wife gave a lunch party in Paris for

4

their old friends the Harold Macmillans. At one point, Dorothy Macmillan turned to Mme de Gaulle and asked in English what she was most looking forward to in retirement.

'A penis,' Mme de Gaulle replied firmly.

The company did not immediately grasp that what she actually meant was ''appiness'.

✡

The late Dame Irene Ward is remembered in the Commons for a question she asked the then Navy Minister about deficiencies in the supply of uniforms to the Women's Royal Naval Service.

The Minister admitted it was so, because the supply of uniforms to male sailors had been given priority.

Dame Irene rose again, deeply irate.

'Is my Right Honourable Friend saying,' she cried, 'that Wrens' skirts must be held up until all the sailors have been satisfied?'

✡

Though ousted from Prime Ministerial office in 1974, Edward Heath continued to travel widely and enjoy the esteem of world statesmen. An early solace for his election defeat was a trip to China and a meeting with Mao Tse-tung, who had always held him in particular regard. The cordiality of their meeting was in no way diminished by the fact that they conversed via an interpreter, on this occasion Prime Minister Chou En Lai.

At one point, Chairman Mao asked Chou En Lai something which caused momentary embarrassment to show on the latter's face.

'What did the Chairman say?' Mr Heath enquired.

'He asked why, when you arrived in Peking, you were not greeted with full state honours. I told him this was because you are no longer leader of your country,' Chou En Lai replied.

At this, Mao spoke again.

'What did he say?' Mr Heath enquired.

'He asked who *is* now the leader of your country.'

'Mr Wilson,' replied Mr Heath.

Mao spoke again, rather more vehemently.

'What did he say?' Mr Heath asked.

'He said "May Mr Wilson stew in eternal shit."'

✣

Harold Wilson's tenure as Prime Minister filled 10 Downing St with the showbiz personalities he doted on — sometimes rather to the exclusion of national and international affairs.

One day, the luncheon guests at No. 10 were playwright John Mortimer and two men from the film division of EMI. During the meal, a secretary entered and whispered urgently in the Prime Minister's ear. It appeared that the regime of Archbishop Makarios had just fallen. Makarios had fled Cyprus to seek asylum in Britain — and was, indeed, shortly to land by helicopter in the back garden of No. 10.

'Show him in,' Mr Wilson said genially.

A few moments later, in full archiepiscopal regalia, towering and outraged, Makarios was ushered up.

'Ah . . . Archbishop Makarios,' Mr Wilson said. 'How are you? I don't think you know John Mortimer. Or these two gentlemen from EMI Films . . .'

✣

President Ronald Reagan's advancing age and far from agile intellect continue to produce moments of sphincter-shrivelling awfulness that resound between the hemispheres.

Most occur when the President's contact-lenses cannot fully make out what is written on the cue cards held up around him. Thus his earnest assertion, in a speech about US aid to underdeveloped countries, that 'America has a very great deal to offer the Third World War'.

Sudden lapses of memory on great public occasions frequently cause the President to become confused about which country he is in, or which foreign statesman he is officially greeting. Arriving in Brasilia last year, he said it was a pleasure to be in 'Bolivia'. When Liberia's President Samuel Doe visited Washington, President Reagan referred to him in the speech of welcome as 'Chairman Moe'. During the banquet marking the State visit of the Prince and Princess of Wales, the President looked straight at Princess Diana and remarked how good it had been at last to make the acquaintance of 'Princess David'.

He is inclined to forget even the names and faces of members of his own Cabinet. The one member who is black arrived at a White House reception for black mayors to be greeted warmly by his president as 'Mister Mayor'.

Still more gruesome instances, however, arise when the President, feeling sprightlier than usual, evades his mental minders for a moment and attempts to improvise. America is still sweating from his radio studio ad lib: 'We start bombing Moscow in five minutes.' An equally spellbinding moment occurred in 1984, just after a terrorist bomb had wiped out a contingent of US Marines at the American Embassy in Beirut. President Reagan, in an unguarded moment, was asked why the embassy's defences had been in so lamentable a state of unreadiness.

'Well . . .' he began in his fireside-story-to-children voice. 'You know how it is when you're fixing up a house . . . It's never ready when you hoped it'd be. Maybe the bathroom still needs painting . . . and you can't get the guy to come and fix the roof . . .' One could see the Secret Service men around him almost burying their faces in their hands.

And who can forget the majesty of presidential language, employed in this description of Libya's Colonel Gadaffi:

'He's not just a barbarian . . . he's flaky.'

✪

When President and Mrs Reagan visited Britain in 1984, a group of children was brought to meet Nancy at London Zoo.

As TV cameras whirred, the dewy-eyed First Lady asked a little boy which animal he'd most liked today.

The little boy replied it had been the chicken he'd had for lunch.

✪

When elected to the Conservative Party leadership in 1975, Margaret Thatcher decided to greet her cheering supporters with a Churchill V-sign.

9

Unfortunately, she delivered it with her fingers the wrong way round.

✿

On her visit to the British Army in the Falkland Islands, Mrs Thatcher was invited to sit on the range-finder's seat of a field-gun.

'Is it safe?' she asked. 'Or will it jerk me off?'

✧

Inspecting a display of garden utensils in a Fulham hardware shop, Mrs Thatcher remarked 'I've never seen a tool as big as that before.'

✧

Speaking at a dinner to mark the retirement of a distinguished Lobby journalist, Mrs Thatcher noted that he had met his wife while 'on the job'.

✧

An exchange of deeply diplomatic language occurred while Mrs Thatcher was visiting India, accompanied by her husband.

At one point, the disgusted Mr Thatcher was prevailed on to don a turban like a massive pink blancmange. As he did so, he was heard to murmur '*Why* won't they ever leave me alone?'

As photographers rushed for the shot, Mr Thatcher protested, 'You're just trying to make me look a bloody fool.'

'No, Mr Thatcher,' a photographer replied, within earshot of all the Indian VIPs. 'It's the bloody natives who are trying to make you look a bloody fool.'

At the height of her 'Buy British' campaign, Mrs Thatcher took to upbraiding journalists who interviewed her about their Japanese tape recorders, and even making them open their jackets to ascertain whether their suits had come from Italy or Hong Kong.

The campaign waned somewhat after the Prime Minister's trip to the Falklands, when it was discovered that the heated hair-rollers she took with her had been made in Denmark.

✧

Even accompanying his wife to China did not, apparently, do much to enlarge Mr Thatcher's global view.

'China,' he was heard to observe later, 'is full of fuck all.'

✧

Returning from Canada with Mrs Thatcher, he vouchsafed to some journalists his observations of that important Commonwealth power:

'Shall I tell you what Canada's full of? It's full of fuck all.'

✧

Near to 10 Downing Street is a small tobacconist's shop which Mr Thatcher frequently patronises.

Recently, he had popped in for 10 Gold Leaf and was popping out again when a woman customer observed to her friend in loud, sympathetic tones:

'You'd think she'd give him enough for 40, so he wouldn't have to come in every day.'

✧

A junior Tory minister was making an impassioned speech about health services at a Commons committee meeting chaired by Lord Hailsham. In mid-flow, he was much disconcerted to hear the Lord Chancellor's voice suddenly exclaim 'Shut up and come and sit on my knee!'

It took everyone a moment to realise that Lord Hailsham was, in fact, addressing his pet dog, Mini.

✧

A very American awful moment occurred at a dinner party given by Robert Kennedy for the Russian poet Yevtushenko during his first visit to America in the Sixties.

The two got on well and when the time came for toasts, Yevtushenko suggested that, after pledging one another, each should hurl his glass into the fireplace, Russian-style.

At this, Kennedy looked worried and held a brief conference with his wife.

'These glasses were a wedding present,' he told Yevtushenko apologetically. 'I hope you won't mind if Ethel gives us some others to throw.'

The alternative goblets were brought. Yevtushenko and Kennedy toasted their new friendship fierily, then each hurled his glass into the fireplace.

But they did not break. They bounced.

✧

When Winston Churchill was Prime Minister, he held a lunch party at 10 Downing Street for some of the day's

14

leading philosophers. Isiah Berlin was one whom he was specially anxious to meet.

The lunch went well though it was noticeable, in the lively philosophical debate which ensued, that very little of a contribution came from Isiah Berlin.

Not until much later was it discovered that Irving Berlin had been invited by mistake.

✿

Long after his retirement, even when enfeebled by two strokes, Churchill would still come into the Commons to listen to debates from his former seat by the gangway.

As he hobbled past one day, a young MP remarked to a friend, 'The old man's getting very gaga, isn't he?'

Churchill turned to them and growled, 'Yes. He's also getting very hard of hearing.'

✿

Malawi's President Hastings Banda is fatally endowed with a boisterous manner and a shocking memory for faces, even royal ones.

On his last visit to Buckingham Palace, he mistook Captain Mark Phillips for Prince Edward, and throughout luncheon kept nudging Princess Anne's husband and exclaiming 'You sure have *grown!*'

✿

On Bob Geldof's Band Aid visit to Sudan in 1985, the head of state, General Swar al Dahab, presented him with one of the country's highest honours, The Order of the Two Niles.

As he received the blue, white and gold insignia, Geldof enquired 'Where are the earrings?'

⭐

Jeremy Thorpe was once hard put to remember the name of the constituent whose hand he was shaking.

'Of course . . .' he beamed as recollection dawned. 'You're Miss Bag.'

The constituent's name was in fact Miss Gas.

⭐

The Rev. Ian Paisley apparently found a new basis for criticising Mrs Thatcher's premiership in a recent TV denunciation of Ulster Secretary Tom King.

'Mr King denies everything!' Mr Paisley thundered. 'He denied there was going to be an Anglo-Irish Agreement — and then his mistress went and signed it on the very next day.'

⭐

Denis Healey's studied lack of further interest in leadership showed a tiny crack — producing an awful moment barely perceptible to the naked eye — when Roy Hattersley mentioned he was going up to Scotland to campaign on the same day as Neil Kinnock.

'Oh?' Mr Healey murmured silkily. 'On the same plane?'

⭐

The magnificent Lord Curzon, on a trip to Paris in the early Twenties, found himself alone for a few minutes before dinner in the hallway of the British Embassy.

As he stood, resplendent in Court dress before the full-length mirror, he was seized by an overwhelming urge to break into a silly little dance.

Turning round a moment later, he saw he was not, after all, alone. The Ambassador's small son was watching him intently through the banisters.

✡

Enoch Powell prides himself on his rapport with Asian immigrants — the more so since his intellectual accomplishments include the ability to speak Urdu.

In the Midlands recently, he strode up to a group of Indian women and addressed them eloquently in Urdu for some time.

The women, being Gujerati, were understandably baffled.

●●●

It is related that a young nobleman at the court of Elizabeth I had the misfortune, while in the Royal earshot, to let out a resounding fart.

Mortified, he fled Gloriana's presence, took ship and set sail for the New World. Over the next few years, he made huge conquests and amassed great fortunes in his monarch's name, driving himself and his men with one aim only — to expiate and expunge the disgrace of that one terrible unguarded moment.

More than a decade later, covered with honour, he returned to London and magnificently presented himself before the Queen.

'Welcome back, my Lord,' she greeted him. 'We had quite forgot the fart.'

Modern British Royalty acknowledges no farts. The essence of majesty is in being deaf and blind to all awful moments — as our Queen demonstrated, smiling on regally at the Maori buttocks constantly flourished at her during her 1986 New Zealand tour. Her forebears have possessed the same talent in even more inscrutable measure.

☆

Listening to a military band at Windsor, Queen Victoria heard a tune she very much liked but could not identify. An equerry was dispatched to the bandmaster to ascertain its title.

He spent some little time rehearsing the tone of voice in which to inform Her Majesty that the tune which had captivated her was Come Where the Booze Is Cheaper.

☆

While staying at Osborne House, Queen Victoria stopped for an impromptu word with an elderly boatman who was getting his skiff ready for the coming season.

'And how's your dear wife?' the Queen kindly enquired.

'Ah,' replied the deaf old salt, patting the hull beside him. 'She'll be all right when we've turned her over and scraped the barnacles off her bottom.'

✧

Edward VII, excellent monarch though he was, had a violent and sometimes uncontrollable temper.

One night at a large Society dinner, the King dropped a speck of spinach on to his starched shirt-front. Uttering an angry bellow, he plunged both hands into the dish and proceeded to plaster all the rest of his ample bosom with spinach.

☆

Edward VII was well known for his indulgence to small children — though it became somewhat strained one day while the King was lunching with his son, the future George V, and his four-year-old grandson, the future Edward VIII and Duke of Windsor.

'Grandpa!' the little boy cried out as the King was speaking. Gently but firmly, he was told he must not interrupt grown-ups' conversation. A moment later, he again shrilled 'Grandpa, Grandpa!'

'You mustn't speak while *I'm* speaking,' the King told him patiently. 'When I've finished speaking, then you'll be allowed to say what you want to.'

A little while later, he turned back to his grandson and said kindly, 'Now — I've finished speaking. What was it you wanted to say?'

'I was going to tell you there was a caterpillar on your lettuce,' the child replied. 'But it's all right — you've eaten it.'

✧

On the Continent, pursuing his numerous amours, Edward VII always travelled under an alias, 'The Duke of Lancaster'. Even so, he expected the deference due to a King.

Calling at a Paris hotel to visit Empress Eugénie, he strode to the elevator with his usual expectation of being made way for. Unfortunately, an American tourist, unaware this was the King of England, plunged for the elevator simultaneously, and the two got stuck fast between its gates.

Bulk and ruthlessness told. The King entered the elevator alone, sending the luckless tourist sprawling out onto the lobby carpet.

✧

Throughout the building of the *Queen Mary*, the Cunard company intended that she should be called the Queen Victoria.

Naturally, formal permission had to be obtained from George V, so two top-hatted Cunard men besought an audience with the King at Buckingham Palace.

'Your Majesty,' one of them began. 'We hope to be permitted to name our new ship after the greatest of all English queens.'

The King fixed him with a steely eye and replied, 'This is a very great honour you are giving my wife.'

✡

The young Anthony Eden, arriving at Buckingham Palace for an audience with George V, was surprised to be received, not in the King's usual study but in a small room at the end of the Palace overlooking the almost constantly active bandstand.

King George apologised, explaining that his study was being redecorated, but adding that the band outside had strict orders not to play until he gave them the signal.

The King then spoke at length about affairs at home and abroad, with particular regard to the League of Nations, which Eden was shortly to attend. At last, a pause arrived, indicating that Eden was expected to supply some observations in return.

As he opened his mouth to begin, the King interrupted, 'Oh — pardon me for a moment', crossed to the window and gave the signal to the band to start playing.

✡

Queen Mary's acquisitiveness was legendary. At any house she was due to visit, the owners would carefully pack all their choicest antique furniture, pictures and ornaments well away out of the Royal sightline. It was a well-established convention that when Queen Mary 'admired' something in her pointed way, she expected to be made a present of it. Buckingham Palace ended up crammed with a huge array of objects prised from their owners by the ruthless gimlet process which Queen Mary called 'caressing with my eyes'.

During the Second World War when Queen Mary was living at Badminton House, there came into her possession a Russian ikon of great beauty but unknown origin. All that its reluctant donor could tell her was that it had come to England some time after the Revolution. Queen Mary took some trouble to establish its proveance, sending it to Sotheby's first, then Christie's, but without success. No one could tell her where the ikon had come from or to whom it had belonged.

Then someone in her Household recollected that there was a Russian princess — a cousin of the British Royal Family — still living in the London suburb whither she had fled to escape the Bolsheviks in 1917. Possibly she would know something about the ikon. Queen Mary concurred and at once wrote to the Princess, inviting her to tea.

The Princess, who had lived 30 years in poverty and obscurity, resigned to the ostracism of her Windsor cousins, was overjoyed. Her joy increased at the tea party, as Queen Mary spoke to her kindly about her parents and relations and the dear dead days under the Tsar. At long last, her wanderings and loneliness seemed to have come to an end. Then Queen Mary brought out the ikon and asked if she knew anything about it.

The Princess took the ikon and pressed it to her heart. She did, indeed, know something about it. She said it was the very ikon given to her at her baptism — the ikon which hung above her bed through her early childhood and to which, each night, she had said her prayers. It was the ikon to which she had prayed for deliverance on the night the Bolsheviks broke into her house, killing her father and mother, her brothers and sisters. It was the ikon she had gone back into the blazing house to rescue, and had carried with her through her long years as a refugee, her sole source of beauty and inspiration until hunger and cold had at last forced her to sell it for a few pennies. Even now, in her illness and despair, its sacred, fragile loveliness still haunted her dreams. The ikon had saved her life. The ikon *was* her life.

'I see,' Queen Mary said, taking the ikon smartly back. 'Thank you *so* much for identifying it.'

✿

During a State visit by the old and short-sighted Queen Olga of The Hellenes, Queen Mary proudly showed off her newest acquisition — a small figure of Lady Godiva on horseback.

'*Dear* Queen Victoria . . .' murmured her guest absent-mindedly.

✿

Queen Mary, in her advancing years, took the wartime

appeal for salvage and scrap iron rather too literally. Driving through the countryside, she would sometimes espy a farmer's plough left out in the fields, and order it to be loaded into her Rolls and taken away for the war effort.

An equerry would be given the ticklish job, next day, of returning the implement to its irate owner.

☆

Queen Mary was terrified of dogs, and lived in fear of the ferocious little Welsh corgis favoured by her granddaughter, the future Elizabeth II. At a Buckingham Palace garden party, Princess Elizabeth handed her a dog biscuit to give to the most ill-tempered of the corgis. Queen Mary in panic handed it on to her nearest neighbour, the Archbishop of Canterbury who, mistaking it for a teatime titbit, gratefully popped it into his mouth.

☆

The Queen Mother's famous good humour can be traced back to the 1940s when, as wife to George VI – in the era when such things were possible – she paid an incognito visit to Harrods Food Hall.

The tail-coated assistant she approached already had a customer, at whose dictation he was writing a long and complicated list in his order-book. Busy as he was, he still showed classic Harrodian courtesy to the evidently important lady, patiently awaiting his attention.

'Good day, Madam,' he said, glancing up, then

returning to his order-book, just a little too soon to see who the lady was.

'Good day,' Queen Elizabeth replied.

'Nice to see you again, Madam,' he said, still writing.

'Thank you,' Queen Elizabeth said.

'Been keeping well, Madam?'

'Very well.'

'And how's your husband?'

'He's well.'

'What's he doing these days?' the assistant enquired, still writing.

'Oh . . .' was the modest reply. '. . . he's still King.'

✧

Out on my regular run through Hyde Park, I was annoyed to have my stride broken by a line of traffic coming along the Serpentine Road at my usual crossing-point.

The last car to approach was a big black limousine. As it passed me, I pulled an irritated face at it and shook my fist.

Then I saw that it contained Her Majesty the Queen.

✧

In the Sixties, just after Princess Margaret married Lord Snowdon, the Queen was introduced to one of London's newly-lionised Cockney fashion photographers.

'Ah,' Her Majesty said. 'I've got a brother-in-law who's a photographer.'

'That's funny,' the Cockney rough diamond replied. 'I've got a brother-in-law who's a queen.'

☆

While lunching with the Queen at Buckingham Palace, Hugh Scanlon attacked a roast potato with such vigour that it shot from his plate on to the floor. As the trade unionist sat blushing, a royal corgi waddled up, sniffed the fallen morsel but disdainfully left it.

'Not your day, is it Mr Scanlon?' Her Majesty commented.

☆

There are times when Royalty can rescue one from awfulness. A publishing friend remembers being at a party where — unknown to her — the Queen was also present and, in fact, standing right next to her. Flinging her arms wide in a conversational gesture, she struck her sovereign full on the bosom.

'Oh Ma'am,' she gasped. 'I'm *so* sorry . . .'

'That's all right my dear,' the Queen replied. 'When you're as small as I am, you're always hitting people in awkward places.'

☆

As Anthony Powell stood in line to receive an honour from the Queen at Buckingham Palace, he heard her say to the man in front of him, 'And what do you do?'

'I kill fleas Ma'am,' was the reply.

'Oh,' said the Queen enthusiastically. 'I'm *so* glad.'

29

Princess Margaret is a more accomplished mimic than she realises.

At a dinner party some years ago, having kept the company in stitches with a whole string of impersonations, she turned to the man on her right and made an observation in her normal voice.

The man dissolved into fresh gales of laughter.

'Oh Ma'am,' he gurgled. 'That's your funniest one of all.'

✿

The Duke of Edinburgh's passion for competitive carriage-driving is rivalled only by his enthusiasm for video equipment.

At one recent international equestrian event which he and the Queen attended, Prince Philip could be seen with yet another new video camera, assiduously recording every entrant and class. When the time came for his own carriage-driving appearance, he asked his then private detective to take over the filming.

Alas, the detective did not realise that the camera had a sound facility, and while filming his master uttered a stream of exasperated and satirical sotto voce comments, as well as making intermittent attempts to chat up a young woman standing next to him.

No one looked at the film until some time later when Prince Philip himself showed it to a gathering of international carriage-driving champions and enthusiasts.

As the stately equipage moved round the show ring with its Royal driver, a voice-over could be heard saying, 'Christ . . . how do you work this thing? . . . All right for tonight are we, darling? . . . Oh Gawd, where's the old bugger got to now? . . .'

✿

Chatting to a *Financial Times* journalist on her Japanese tour, the Princess of Wales, somewhat surprisingly, expressed enthusiasm for that most sober and serious organ.

'I love the *FT*,' she said. 'We always had it at home. I used to line the bottom of my hamster's cage with it.'

✿

When the Prince and Princess of Wales met the Pope in 1984, things were made a little sticky by the latter's extremely limited English. At that time, His Holiness's vocabulary did not go much beyond 'Yes' and his all-purpose, beaming, smiling 'Congratu*lations*!'

Princess Charles took the conversational initiative by remarking, 'It must have been *awful* to be shot.'

'Yes,' the Pope agreed benignly.

Moved by the recollection of that terrible event — as well as the obvious need for sign-language — Princess Diana put a hand on her stomach and gave a wince.

At this, understanding shone in the Pope's eyes.

'Congratu*lations*!' he beamed.

✿

The moment most awfully lacking finesse on Prince Charles's visit to Dallas occurred when one of the city's leading oil barons was given the honour of escorting the Royal visitor into a cocktail party.

'Boys . . .' the oil baron said. 'This is the Prince of Wales . . . Prince of Wales — these are the boys.'

☆

A party game much enjoyed by Prince Andrew in his bachelor days was a hooraying variant of blind man's buff. A young lady would be blindfolded and then try to identify each male guest by feeling his anatomy.

During one such revel, the blindfolded female dived under a table, suspecting one of her quarry to be hiding there. Reaching out, she felt a large, tweed-covered bottom.

'Steady on,' she heard a voice say. 'H.R.H. here.'

• • •

Mrs M. Joseph of Whitefield, Manchester, was standing in a check-out queue at her local supermarket one busy evening. As her turn approached, the person behind her thrust a single tin of dog food in front of her and said 'I've only got this. Do you think I could go ahead of you?'

Mrs Joseph felt justifiable irritation at this failure to use the nearby 'express' check-out, for few or single purchases. 'All right,' she said, without turning round. 'But you do know there are special queues for people like you . . .'

A sharp intake of breath made her turn round. The young man with the tin of dog food was black.

✡

The most deliberately prepared awful moment was probably that which awaited all who entered the presence of Peter the Great.

Before they could speak to the monarch, they had to drink a pint of sherry, handed to them by a trained bear.

✡

The late Sir Iain Moncreiffe of that Ilk had many disconcerting habits. While with Hugh Cawdor in the bar at White's Club, he suddenly took out his false teeth and made snapping motions with them over a bowl of cocktail olives.

Replacing the teeth, he smiled at a dumbfounded neighbour and explained, 'That's my butterfly. It wanted an airing, you see.'

The most common awful moment in literary life is to meet an author one had loved and revered, and to discover him or her to be just another fallible human being, prone like anyone else to bad breath, bad temper and bogeys on the nose. The classic example was an evening in the Twenties when Marcel Proust and James Joyce happened to be together in one room. The entire company fell silent and strained forward to overhear the tremendous encounter. But all the two giants of 20th century literature did was talk about their sciatica.

The awfulness in authorship would require a volume to itself. How to reply with any semblance of politeness to the question 'Do you write under your own name?' How not to doze off when someone says 'Do you think up your own ideas . . . ?' How to explain, even to close loved ones, that it is *not* a hobby, like making galleons from match-sticks. How not to shoot or strangle people who believe that interrupting you at work cheers you up. While Nik Cohn slaved at his typewriter against a deadline, his cleaning lady would now and again push open the door and playfully call out 'Tap tap tap'.

Nor should it ever be thought that when a book is finished, awfulness ends. I hear of an American writer whose latest novel, an almost certain best-seller, was waiting shipment in a warehouse in New England. A heavy rainstorm arose. The warehouse roof collapsed, and the entire edition of the novel was submerged. Then intense cold set in. The rainwater froze, entombing the books in ice.

✿

To celebrate the birthday of a prominent London publisher, his staff had planned a surprise party, to be sprung on him when he arrived home in the evening. Thirty-odd people, with champagne and carnival streamers, hid themselves beyond the arch of the handsome two-room library whither, without fail each evening, the publisher came to read his paper and day's correspondence.

Utterly unaware of their presence, the great man entered, settled himself in his favourite chair, opened his paper and, believing himself comfortably alone, lifted up one buttock and let out a loud, langurous fart.

✧

Ved Mehta is revered for the courage with which, handicapped by blindness, he made his way from India to New York and literary fame. But he is not always the most agreeable of men. It is his habit, when introduced to someone at a party, to make some remark like 'What a pretty red dress', compounding the discomfiture his blindness and fragility can create. It has even been suggested in some quarters that he may not really be blind at all, and that all his harrowing tales of hardship and fortitude in *The New Yorker* are just an elaborate literary con.

A certain New York editor was fascinated by the possibility. Arriving at a party and espying a familiar Asian figure in the corner, he decided to put the matter to the test once and for all. Stationing himself before the familiar Asian figure, he stuck his fingers in the corners of his mouth and pulled a grotesquely childish face. The familiar Asian figure stared at him blankly. The editor goggled his eyes, waggled his ears and stuck out his tongue as far as it would go. The familiar Asian figure continued to stare at him blankly.

At this point, his hostess came up, guided him away by one elbow and inquired:

'Why on earth are you pulling those terrible faces at V. S. Naipaul?'

✩

At another New York party some years ago, the author William Burroughs decided to recreate the story of William Tell by putting a glass of gin on his wife's head and shooting it off with a revolver.

He missed, and shot his wife dead.

✩

When Thomas Hardy died in 1928, his will directed that he be buried unostentatiously in the churchyard at Stinsford, deep in his beloved Wessex. However, just before the funeral, a suggestion came from Stanley Baldwin's government that so great a novelist and poet — whatever his own wishes — deserved no less a burial-place than Westminster Abbey.

Between Hardy's widow and the government, a compromise was reached. The great man's body would be interred at Westminster — but first his heart would be removed and, in a private ceremony following the public one, be buried at its symbolic home, Stinsford.

There then arose the question of who should remove

PUSS
of the d'Urbervilles

the heart. Hardy's family doctor refused, but a young assistant volunteered in his stead. The heart was cut out at the surgery, and the body taken away to London for burial with national honours.

Since the heart was not to be buried until the next day, some method of storing it had to be found. Finally, the doctor's maid, one Nellie Titterington, came up with the answer — a biscuit-tin.

The biscuit-tin was sealed and placed in a garden-shed to await the morrow's poignant and poetic interrment of Thomas Hardy's heart. Unluckily, during the night it was got at by the doctor's cat.

✥

After Lytton Strachey had published his classic biography of Queen Victoria in 1921, he received a summons to Buckingham Palace.

He went in some excitement, naturally supposing he was to be offered some honour for his work.

He was shown into a small, gloomy sitting room. After a moment, a Court official entered, briefly corrected one point of fact in the book and exited, leaving Strachey to see himself out.

✥

During the Second World War, Evelyn Waugh was talking to a friend who had managed to get out of Japan just before hostilities commenced, but had been obliged to leave his Japanese wife behind.

'Now I suppose,' Waugh said, 'she's been raped by a hundred Japanese soldiers.'

'Yes,' was the reply.

✥

Brendan Behan, the roistering Irish playwright, made many heroic attempts to get off the bottle that was eventually to kill him.

His longest dry spell lasted some months — and, indeed, seemed to have been so successful that a London temperance league invited him to be guest speaker at their annual meeting. Behan accepted and, since the invitation stipulated evening dress, soberly went to Moss Bros to hire himself a dinner jacket.

Unluckily, the hour at which he set off to the temperance meeting happened to be 6pm — the moment when pub lights twinkle on invitingly. The temptation was finally too much. Behan stopped with his taxi-driver for a quick one, and never resumed his journey.

He came to next morning in the gutter, still wearing the Moss Bros dinner jacket. In his night's wanderings, he vomited over it, and both urinated and defecated in it. Since it was clearly beyond drycleaning or fumigation, Behan simply dug a hole in his garden and buried it.

Some months later, an elderly assistant at Moss Bros looked in the hire-book and saw that the garments hired to a Mr B. Behan were still outstanding. He therefore dispatched a polite note, asking for their return at Mr Behan's convenience. Unfortunately, the note reached Behan just as he was falling off the wagon again. He went out into his garden, dug up the dinner jacket, put it back into its box, wrapped the tissue paper round it and sent it back to Moss Bros.

✥

The novelist Clemence Dane could make whole rooms full of her friends shrivel with embarrassment over her blithe and booming *double entendres*. 'Come to dinner,' she once hallooed down the phone to Arthur Marshall. 'I've got a pair of really wonderful cocks . . .'

Marshall remembers shrinking into the corner of a taxi as Clemence pronounced at the top of her voice on the Shakespeare-Bacon controversy.

'I believe Shakespeare sucked Bacon dry. Not that Bacon *minded* being sucked . . .'

✿

It is every author's nightmare to lose the single manuscript copy of whatever book he is currently writing. When authors are burgled, their first anguished cry will not be about the silver or hi-fi: it will be 'Is my book safe?'

Laurens van der Post suffered the nightmare of nightmares, returning to his ransacked house to find the burglars had used the pages of his manuscript to wrap up the things they were stealing.

✿

In the mid-Seventies, the Oxford University Press acknowledged their large sales in African countries by commissioning a study of the abundant plant-life in the Kenya highlands.

As the book was going to press, a sharp-eyed editor hurriedly amended its original title. Had this not been done, the OUP's stately list of acronyms — *OED* and the rest — would have been adorned by a work entitled *Flora of Upper Kenya*.

✿

On assignment in America in the Seventies, I was entertained to tea by two enormously stout Mormon ladies. During conversation, they elicited the fact that I had just published my first novel.

'Oh, how exciting,' one of these two truly massive, but very kind and delightful women said. 'We must order it. What's its title?'*

✿

A young man invited to lunch with Sir Harold Nicolson strove for a Nicolsonian epigram when his host mildly asked his opinion of a certain mutual acquaintance.

'*Terrible* chap,' the young man drawled, ' — the sort of person who offers you South African sherry.'

He did not notice that Sir Harold, at that very moment, was pouring him a glass of South African sherry.

✿

The late, much-lamented Truman Capote was in a New York restaurant on one of those rare latter nights which found him both sober and undrugged. He was, of course, instantly recognised and a succession of female admirers came across to his table to eulogise his work and offer match-books and paper napkins for him to sign.

The husband of one of them objected that feminine emotion should be wasted thus on a self-confessed homosexual. He himself came across, unzipped his fly

* The title of my first novel was Slip On A Fat Lady

43

and hung his penis out under Capote's nose. 'Maybe you'd like to sign this,' he suggested.

Capote inspected the dangling member politely.

'I don't know if I can sign it,' he said. 'Maybe I could just *initial* it . . .'

☆

The writer and naturalist Richard Mabey was walking through a field with a friend, discoursing in his usual rapt fashion about the flowers and grasses all around.

Suddenly, it seemed to the friend that Mabey, without any warning, executed an Olympic-style long jump from beside him to a point about 15 feet ahead.

Only on turning round did he realise that the unfortunate naturalist had been tossed thither by a bull.

☆

Earlier this year, the literary agent David Bolt was interviewed on radio about his just-published *Authors' Handbook*.

'How important to an author is presentation?' the interviewer asked.

'*Very* important,' Mr Bolt replied. 'The order and presentation of material is just about the most important part of being successful as an author.'

'Just talk us through the chapters of your book then, will you?'

'Yes,' Mr Bolt said. 'Only, they're not in the order I originally had them. The publisher sent my first draft back and made me change it.'

✧

Christopher Logue and the painter Derek Boshier were on their way to see the publisher of a silk screen print on which they had collaborated. The publisher's office was in South Kensington and it happened to be a spring day when the streets lay under drifts of fallen cherry blossom.

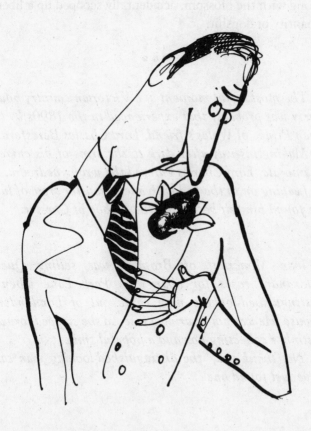

As artist and poet approached, their publisher — a very correct and well-dressed man — came out of his door into the street to greet them. Christopher Logue impetuously snatched up a double handful of blossom from the pavement and flung it over the dapper figure in a shower of poetical celebration and gratitude.

It would have been more poetical still had he not, along with the blossom, accidentally scooped up a liberal quantity of dogshit.

•••

The most awful moment at a Victorian country house party was probably that experienced in the 1890s by the then Prince of Wales's friend, Lord Charles Beresford.

Making his way after dark to the arms of his current inamorata, Lord Charles entered the wrong bedroom.

Leaping on to the bed with a wild rooster crow of lust, he found himself bestriding the Bishop of Chester.

✿

Joan Moncrieff of Bromley was selling Queen Alexandra roses for charity in Park Lane when a distinguished-looking man came out of Londonderry House. He was not wearing a rose, so she stepped forward with her collecting-box and a hopeful smile.

'No, thank you,' the distinguished-looking man said. 'I've just found one.'

✿

The original draft of America's Star Wars strategy had to be recalled for further work when President Reagan's scientists realised they had omitted one small fact from their calculations.

They had not taken into account that the Earth is round.

✩

A girl recently left Trevor Sorbie's Covent Garden hair salon with ashen punk spikes as long as the Statue of Liberty's.

As she crossed the piazza, a pigeon flew into her hair and got stuck.

SHOW BUSINESS

Show business revels in its embarrassments as a kind of narcissism. I can scarcely describe the loathing I feel for the kind of stories actors always tell about funny things on the stage or set with 'Larry' and 'Johnny', the punchline barely detectable in washes of glutinous false affection. Still less can I describe my feelings towards the sycophantic journalists and broadcasters who perpetuate them. Recently on *Start the Week*, Sheridan Morley could be heard yet again ululating the tired old one about Ralph Richardson that ends with the line (yawn) 'If you think I'm drunk, wait till you see the Duke of Buckingham'. I swear on my honour it does not appear — nor anything like it — in the section following.

✧

During the 1960s, a Hollywood producer had the idea of bringing back Busby Berkeley to choreograph a modern musical with the choral extravaganzas he had brought to such a surrealistic art in musicals of the Thirties.

Busby Berkeley was now a very old man but, the producer's aides reported, extremely alert mentally and keen to do the project. He was asked to supply the studio with a full list of what he would require to stage the choral routine of his dreams.

The list, as expected, called for some hundreds of swimming chorus girls and dozens of white grand pianos, but ended with a rather puzzling item: 'Twelve trained eagles'.

The producer called up Busby Berkeley — who sounded, as reported, a very alert old gentleman — and said the list was fine, but why did he need the twelve trained eagles?

He said he wanted them so that, at the end of the routine, they could swoop down and carry off the twelve leading chorus girls in their beaks.

✧

The Beatles' former road manager Mal Evans was accidentally shot dead by police in the bedroom of a Los Angeles motel. The motel subsequently sent his widow in England a bill for the cost of cleaning the carpet.

✧

It may not be generally realised that Sylvester Stallone wears built-up shoes. At a Hollywood awards dinner last year, the macho star found his shoes paining him, so he discreetly slipped them off under the table.

When the time came to leave, he discovered they had vanished — stolen by a souvenir hunter.

There was no choice but for Rambo to exit in stockinged feet, some inches shorter than when he had entered.

✧

When Hollywood bought a certain scandalous Sixties best-seller, much agonising took place at script conferences about how much of the book's sexual frolicking could be shown on screen. One scene in particular bothered the studio boss — that in which the hero was described lying in his bath, being urinated on by six women.

'That's gotta go,' he told the scriptwriters. 'We *can't* show a guy being urinated on by six women.'

'It's important to the story,' a scriptwriter demurred.

'Okay,' the studio boss said, 'but can't we make it just *four* women?'

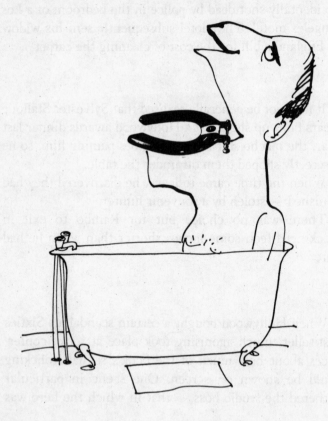

✿

Sir Thomas Beecham was a master of finely-tuned crushingness and belittlement.

One day, he met the drama critic James Agate just after Agate had published a book of essays called *Buzz Buzz*.

'I see you've got a book out,' Beecham said. 'It's called Buzz . . . I can't remember the rest of the title . . .'

✿

The filming of a Second World War epic a few years ago featured an actor whose vibrant homosexuality does not stop him from specialising in tough guy roles, as Gestapo interrogators or sadistic POW camp commandants.

During filming on location in Austria, the actor conceived a passion for a young assistant director, but managed to suppress it right up until the final day, when everyone was checking out of the location hotel.

At the reception desk, the young assistant director could be heard fretting about the quantity of his hand-baggage and how difficult it would make showing his travel documents at the airport.

'Oh — I guess I'll manage,' he said. 'When I go through passport control, I'll just have to hold two cases in one hand and put my camera-bag between my legs.'

From an armchair across the lobby, a wistful voice sighed:

'Oh . . . I vish you vould put *me* between your legs!'

✿

The casting director who chose Victor Mature to play Samson in Cecil B. DeMille's *Samson and Delilah* could hardly have found a less suitable tower of strength. During filming it emerged that Mature was afraid of water, afraid of crowds and afraid of heights. He was afraid of the tame lion his stand-in had to grapple with, and afraid of the fake swords used in the battle scenes. In the sequence when Samson slays the Philistines with an ass's jawbone, he even took fright at the studio wind-machine, and fled to his dressing-room in terror.

DeMille had him brought back and, in front of the assembled cast and technicians, made the following speech:

'I have met a few men in my time. Some have been afraid of heights, some have been afraid of water, some have been afraid of fire, some have been afraid of closed spaces. Some have even been afraid of open spaces — or themselves. But in all my thirty-five years of picture-making experience, Mr Mature, I have not until now met a man who was 100 per cent yellow.'

✽

During the Fifties, the regular followers of Mick Mulligan's jazz band included a girl named Barbara, famed for the weary adeptness with which she had resisted the attempts of nearly all the band, at various times, to get her into bed.

One night, the Mulligan band was playing at the Slade School of Art. At the formal reception beforehand,

Barbara was introduced to the principal, Sir William Coldstream.

'I may as well tell you straight away,' she said as she shook Sir William's hand. 'I don't fuck.'

☆

When Madam Chiang Kai Shek visited MGM studios in the Thirties, Samuel Goldwyn greeted her with the words: 'I guess I should have brought along my laundry.'

On a later occasion, playing tennis doubles against the King of Siam, Goldwyn was repeatedly to be heard urging his partner: 'Hit it harder to the Chink.'

☆

The birthday of a top British rock star coincided with his setting off on a world tour including, not only America and Australia but also out-of-the-way places like Hong Kong, Thailand, Singapore and Indonesia.

At the lavish birthday-cum-farewell party thrown for the star by his record company, someone had the hilarious idea of decorating the birthday cake with joke candles — the kind which, when blown out, flicker mischievously on again.

The party foregathered, the rock star and his entourage arrived and, as a fitting climax to the evening of ego-massaging, the birthday cake was wheeled in, its candles burning brightly.

The rock star stepped forward amid cheers and blew them out. They came on again. There was a faint titter.

The star blew the candles out again, and again they came on. There was a louder titter.

The star blew out the candles a third time, and on they came again. This time, the titter changed to loud guffaws — which died into mortified silence as the rock star turned on his heel and walked out.

Next day, the world tour — to America, Australia, Hong Kong, Singapore and Indonesia — was cancelled.

✿

The most awful moment preserved on a gramophone record is to be found on the 'live' LP where Jack Jones sings the hippie song 'Everything Is Beautiful', and accidentally gets one line back to front.

The result is an appeal for brotherly love more vivid than the composer could ever have meant:

'We shouldn't care about the colour of his hair . . . or the length of his skin.'

✿

On his first visit to New York, Robert Helpmann was pirouetting along Broadway, winsomely attired in trilby and spats, carrying gloves and a cane. Suddenly, a huge construction worker blocked his path and snarled 'Ya goddammed fuckin' fairy!'

Helpmann lifted his cane, pointed it at the man and, in his best fairy voice, said 'Vanish!'

✿

During the Rolling Stones' notorious stay at Hugh

Hefner's Playboy Mansion in 1972, Mick Jagger's seigneurial eye fell on a girl named Bobbie Arnstein, formerly a Playboy Bunny and girlfriend of Hefner, now relegated to being the Great Swinger's 'personal assistant'.

Her varied life with Hefner had made Bobbie Arnstein, unhappily, a victim of *anorexia nervosa*. When the Stones arrived, she had just come to the end of a period of self-starvation which was about to result in its inevitable consequence, an eating binge. Unaware of Jagger's interest, she gorged a vast dinner, ending with Stilton cheese and onions. Then, while the Stones revelled downstairs, she retired to bed, taking with her a large slice of Black Forest gâteau in case she felt hungry again during the night.

In the early hours of the morning, she answered a tap on her door. There stood Mick Jagger, wearing a pair of skin-tight white leather trousers.

Bobbie Arnstein faced an exquisite dilemma, wishing to succumb to Jagger's advances but at the same time not wanting him to get within range of her oniony breath. She further wished to divert his attention from the slice of Black Forest gâteau, which she had left unromantically reposing on a chair.

Her apparent reluctance made Jagger grow still more ardent. Unluckily, in the scuffle, she fended him off a little too roughly. He lost his balance, staggered back and, in his white leather trousers, sat heavily down on the Black Forest gâteau.

✥

The most awful moment ever seen in a British film occurs in that fine Ealing war drama, *The Cruel Sea*.

The film's most harrowing sequence shows Jack Hawkins as corvette Captain Ericson faced with a terrible dilemma. He suspects the German U-boat he is hunting to be hiding under the survivors of a torpedoed British merchantman. He takes the horrendous decision to drop depth-charges, even though it will mean killing the British sailors to be seen even now shouting and waving joyfully to him as their rescuer.

There is no U-boat. The next scene, from the corvette's stern, shows nothing in the sea but dead sailors, a little debris and the wheeling gulls whose cries bear witness to the tragedy.

The episode was filmed by two camera-units — the first going towards the scene, the second leaving it behind. Unfortunately, however, something went wrong in the second unit, and they missed their stern shot altogether. There was no way of retaking the scene. All that could be done, when editing-time came, was to run the approach shot in reverse. It seemed safe enough since sea and sky look much the same moving either way.

Only one little detail went unnoticed. In all the years that haunting aftermath to Captain Ericson's mistake has been seen on cinema and TV screen, no one has ever wondered why all the seagulls are flying backwards.

✧

An American cowboy star, famous for his sanctimonious good influence on children, used to vary his movie roles with guest appearances in galas and circuses, riding the famous, equally virtuous horse on which he was wont to chase bad men across the screen.

On the eve of one such circus appearance, before a crowd to be mainly made up of children, the cowboy star found one of his accompanying musicians drunk, and summarily fired him.

The man took an imaginative revenge. Just before the circus parade, he crept into the horse's stall and, by means neither recorded nor imaginable, managed to give the animal an erection.

Horses' erections, if unappeased, do not go away for hours. The cowboy star had no option but to ride his steed in that condition, out in front of the thousands of children.

●●●

There are people with a gift for 'passing remarks' (to use a plangent old fashioned phrase) which induce, even in moderate and forgiving temperaments, a sincere desire to hammer them into the earth with an outsize mallet. The strange thing about these artists in verbal hemlock is that, very often, no harm is meant. The intention can be a compliment — though the way it comes out makes a poinard in the back infinitely preferable.

Sir John Gielgud is a celebrated exponent. Visiting the young Richard Burton during his debut as Hamlet, Sir

John found him suffering from a heavy cold. 'I'll look in and see you again when you're better,' the great actor said kindly. 'I mean in health of course.'

When Brigid Keenan left The Observer *after a highly successful career as woman's editor, David Astor told her 'We shall miss your little piccolo in our great orchestra.' Felicity Green remembers being told by an apparently sincere friend, 'You're so lucky. You're small enough to be able to get away with wearing really cheap clothes.'*

Compliments like double doses of prussic acid tend to issue most lethally from mothers-in-law. A young wife I know, having been on chronically bad terms with her in-laws, decided to set things straight by cooking them a magnificent dinner. At the conclusion of the meal, her mother-in-law looked across the table at her and said judicially, 'Yes . . . I think we can give you back your stripes.'

The prize, in any department, goes to the Jewish mother of a friend of mine, when he took his first wife — who was not Jewish — home for a weekend that happened to coincide with Passover. At breakfast, in place of bread, her new mother-in-law offered her a Mazza biscuit.

'I won't, thank you,' she replied. 'I find they make me a bit constipated.'

'No one would think so,' her mother-in-law replied levelly, 'considering the amount of lavatory paper that's been used in this house over the past two days.'

Broadcasting

Some years ago on American network TV, the wife of a golf champion told her interviewer that before every big match she always wished her husband good luck by kissing his balls. The interviewer did not laugh — did not even smile — but proceeded to the next question with not so much as a tremor in his voice. The episode is held up as a supreme example of professionalism and self-discipline in broadcasting.

Discipline actually has little to do with it. The strange fact about most professional broadcasters is that they are terrified of broadcasting. All that ever concerns them on the air is getting through the next five minutes, somehow. In their mesmerised self-absorption, they scarcely notice their interviewees or register what replies are given to their questions. There is, besides, a reflex common to all radio and TV people — reflecting both the immensity and evanescence of their medium — when such awful moments occur. It reminds me of the Arabian Nights story where a bridegroom farts in the bridal chamber and all the women chatter and jingle their ornaments, resolutely pretending it never happened.

✧

This Bridal Chamber method was demonstrated richly and at length on the American late night chat show hosted by — the word has no comic overtones in America — Alan Thicke.

Mr Thicke's guests one night included an 'exotic actress', famed for her many roles in 'adult movies' — i.e. a porn queen. The purpose of the interview was to inquire seriously into her craft and its harmfulness, or otherwise, to Society. All Thicke's questions could produce, however, were ghastly *double entendres* in galloping chain reaction: 'Thank you for coming . . .' 'Thank you for having me . . .' 'Tell me the tricks of your trade . . .' 'I'm just an ordinary pro' . . .' As bad as it got, neither interviewer nor guest quite gave way to laughter. The studio audience meanwhile sat in what can only be described as an audible palsy.

Wild-eyed with pent-up hysteria, Alan Thicke made a last desperate attempt to be serious. Exotic movies, he said, were not so different from ordinary movies, were they? The directors of sex scenes might still be *good* directors, might they not?

'Oh sure,' his guest agreed. 'Though it looks as if I'm making it with a guy in bed, I'm still acting . . . The director's got to know how to pull that little something out of me . . .'

✿

BBC-TV's *Rough Justice* programme became deservedly famous for its campaign on behalf of Terence Mycock, the man convicted of a burglary that never took place. The conclusive moment in the campaign was an appearance on camera by Lord Denning. The former Lord Chief Justice declared that if he had been trying the case, he would never have sent Terence Mycock to jail.

'Lord Denning,' his interviewer said . . . and paused dramatically. 'Would you like to see Mycock set free?'

✿

During the mid-Sixties, the BBC's Michael Barratt was refereeing a television debate between representatives of Rhodesia's two freedom movements, Zanu and Zapu. Picking up a point raised by one of them, Barratt interjected, 'That's all very well — but two blacks don't make a white . . .'

☆

A television discussion was in progress about the South American air crash in which the survivors had turned to cannibalism. One of the experts was asked whether even such extremes of hunger could justify the devouring of human flesh.

'Well,' he began cautiously. 'I think they started off on the wrong foot . . .'

✪

A memorable over in Test cricket began when the BBC commentator reminded his listeners:

'The bowler's Holding, the batsman's Willey . . .'

✪

BBC-TV had a correspondent on board HMS *Tiger*, the British warship used for top secret talks between Harold Wilson and Rhodesia's recalcitrant Ian Smith in 1965.

In his first dispatch, the BBC man reported that both statesmen were now on board, though they had arrived too late in the evening to get down to any serious negotiating. 'But it is known,' the bulletin continued, 'that Mr Wilson and Mr Smith had a short, friendly talk before they went to bed.'

✪

BBC-TV's Michael Buerk sought for a pithy sign-off to an item about the boycotted 1986 South African athletics games.

'Nobody wants to play with the South Africans,' he said. 'So for these next two weeks they'll have to play with themselves.'

☆

Lynne Reid-Banks became famous as one of the most innocent as well as one of the earliest female reporters on ITV.

Interviewing the wife of a European monarch famous for lavish entertaining, she inquired 'Does your husband have big balls?'

On another occasion, she was sent to talk to children after their injections of a new polio vaccine.

'Have you all had Smarties?' Ms Reid-Banks asked.

'Yes,' the children answered.

'I haven't had any,' she told them, 'because I haven't had my prick yet.'

☆

Ted Lowe, the BBC's snooker commentator, was describing a certain star whom middle age had begun to prevent from playing the full range of gymnastic shots the table allows.

'He can't get his leg over any more,' Lowe whispered. 'So he's having to rely on using that left hand . . .'

☆

A chat show on local radio began as usual by 'trailing' the studio guests to be interviewed that morning by himself and his female co-presenter.

'. . . We shall also be hearing from our resident psychologist — who's across the table with Sandra . . .'

☆

Like most TV companies, London Weekend Television keeps a board in their reception area, announcing which shows or programmes are in the process of being recorded.

Arriving at LWT a few years ago to record his Saturday chat show, Russell Harty was peeved to find written on the announcement board: 'London Weekend Television Present Russel Harty Plus.'

He went to the commissionaire at the reception desk and pointed out that his first name should be spelt with two ls. The man looked in his store of stick-on letters and replied that there were no more ls.

'I am Russell Harty,' the star expostulated, 'and I want my name spelt right!'

When he came out through the foyer later, the board had been amended. It now read: ' ondon Weekend Television Presents RusselL Harty Plus.'

✫

The BBC's ineluctable Brian Johnston on a batsman retired hurt but sportingly returning to finish the over:

'What a good show! I don't think he's too badly hurt . . . one ball left.'

✫

Interviewing Niki Lauda, not long after an escape from a blazing Grand Prix car had left him terribly scarred, Pete Murray inquired, 'Do you have any burning ambitions left, Niki?'

✿

'Now a song from Elvis Presley — who's got a lot of living to do.'

Ken Bruce, Radio 2

✿

During BBC Television's first-ever Party Political Broadcast in 1951, presenter Macdonald Hobley introduced, on the Conservative side, Mr Anthony Eden and, on Labour's side, 'Sir Stifford Crapps'.

●●●

A furniture-restorer friend had almost completed the meticulous refurbishment of an Elizabethan mahogany sideboard. The only imperfection remaining was an empty space among the row of intricately-carved rosettes along its back.

The furniture-restorer searched every antique-shop he knew for such a mahogany rosette, but to no avail. Then, walking home one night, to his utter amazement, he saw that exact pattern of rosette lying on the pavement.

Joyfully he picked it up.

It was dogshit.

✿

Shortly after the Normandy landings, Allied troops entered a town whose main square was pleasantly lined with pavement cafés, all open for business.

As two or three British officers sat in the sun, enjoying their coffee and brandy, they noticed a group of officers outside the café directly opposite, doing the same. 'I wonder what regiment those other chaps belong to,' someone said idly.

Only then did it dawn on them that the 'other chaps' were not uniformed in khaki but in German field grey ...

☆

There is a wealthy old lady in Palm Beach with an extraordinary history. In the Twenties, her daughter went on holiday to Hawaii, and was brutally raped. The lady herself then went to Hawaii, found the rapist and shot him dead. At her trial, she was represented by Clarence Darrow, later famous as defence counsel in the Scopes 'Monkey Trial'. The upshot was that Darrow got her acquitted.

The story switches to a few years ago when a policeman in Palm Beach saw the wealthy old lady drive by with no tax disc displayed on her Rolls-Royce.

When he stopped her, she produced the disc from the glove-compartment, apologising profusely for not having fixed it to the windscreen. The policeman said he'd have to make out a report, though he was sure there wouldn't be any prosecution.

He took down her name and address and then, apologetically — for she was such a very old, wealthy and well-known Palm Beach lady — inquired whether she had any previous violations.

'Yes,' she replied. 'Murder One.'

✿

Felicity Green witnessed a unique sartorial awful moment at a West End theatre just before curtain-up. A man in an old-fashioned dinner jacket was making his way along a row, behind a lady whose hair was arranged in an elaborate chignon. As he passed her, his protuberant fly buttons and her chignon became caught fast.

✿

A female acquaintance, on a first date with a man she much fancied, was gratified to be told as they sat down to dinner: 'You remind me of someone. I can't think who it is.'

All through a romantic meal, he kept saying she reminded him of someone, but he couldn't think who. Was it Raquel Welch, she wondered? Or possibly Madonna?

As they got up to leave, the dream man suddenly exclaimed: 'I know who it is you remind me of! Bernard Cribbins!'

✿

Food has been an infallible source of awful moments for me since childhood. Oh, those gorge-rising ordeals of meat-fat, gristle, yellow broad beans, school cabbage and hard potato! Up to the age of 10, the only things I really liked were baked beans and cherryade. I assumed, moreover, that households other than ours had never heard of these things, and that if I so much as went to tea with another boy, there would be fat or fish-skin involved, and I would be obliged to eat it.

Staying overnight with a school friend, I was asked if I'd like puffed wheat for supper. I had no idea of what it was, but said yes resignedly and began to crunch my way through the bowlful in grim determination. Then I saw my hostess looking rather oddly at me.

'Don't you want any milk on them?' she said.

Childhood cannot compete, of course, with the awful moments visited on grown-ups, whether in restaurants or their own kitchens. I count it among my true blessings that I never learned to cook, and so was spared at least those dangerous passions and risks. The only thing I've ever really cooked is my face-flannel. I was boiling it to clean it, and got called away to the telephone. I returned half an hour later to find, not only the face-flannel but the whole saucepan missing. All that remained was a sheet of molten metal covering the stove-top and, in the middle, a small lozenge of ash.

Perhaps you'd better think twice about coming to dinner here.

✿

That fine English maître Bill Lacey some years ago attended an international gathering of chefs, restaurateurs and food writers in Switzerland. The climax was a party at which each famous chef publicly cooked one dish for the assembled gourmets. Lacey decided on classic simplicity — a perfect roast chicken, cooked on an open fire in an earthenware 'brick'.

During the cooking, he was called away to the other side of the room. Unable to escape his interlocutors, he saw to his consternation that every waiter who passed the chicken was energetically basting it with scalding gravy. As he watched, still unable to escape, he saw its earthenware brick begin to glow red-hot.

The final dousing of gravy was too much. With a huge bang, the earthenware brick exploded, the roast chicken flew through the air and landed inside a chandelier.

✡

In the Seventies, you could buy a brand of Irish sausages whose packet warranted that they were 'Eight thick sausages'.

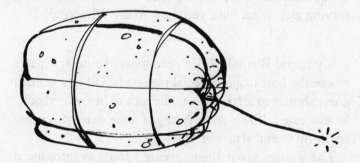

73

A female acquaintance was lunching with a journalist from the lower end of Fleet Street, a gentleman usually happier with a pint of wallop at the pub.

'They do wine en carafe here,' my friend observed.

'That's fine,' her companion assented. 'I'll have a glass of carafe.'

☆

There is a restaurant in Kent whose chef-proprietor, some years ago, decided to offer his patrons the medieval dish of wild boar.

A wild boar was brought from France and housed in the restaurant's grounds which, fortunately, were spacious. No one, however, was prepared for the ticklish job of butchering it. During the attempt, the boar escaped from its enclosure, charged into the house and ran amok through the crowded restaurant.

☆

Even as I write, there is a new Burger King radio commercial in which a young man asks the Burger King serving girl 'What have you done to my Whopper?'

☆

My friend Russell Miller remembers being at a party where the host made a special plea on behalf of a woman guest shortly to arrive. '*Please* be nice to her, everybody,' he entreated. 'She's *terribly* shy. *Please* don't do or say anything to embarrass or upset her.'

The woman guest then appeared and was introduced

amid understandable tension and circumspection. One of the men picked up a bowl of pistachio nuts and offered it to her. She took a handful and, not seeing the kind of nuts they were, put them straight into her mouth.

Forbidden to say anything that might embarrass her, the company watched spellbound while she crunched her way through the whole lot, shells and all.

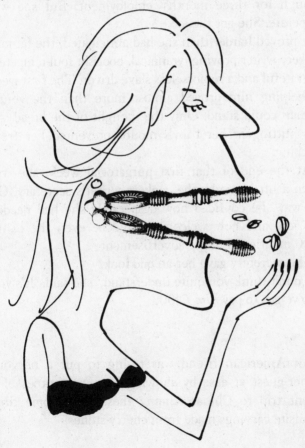

✿

'Wanted' — ran a small ad in *The Times*. 'Assistant for famous cookery writer. Three-month contract: £400.'

The ad was answered by a young woman, recently widowed and with a young baby, desperate for work of any kind. The hours were long, and £400 seemed little enough for three months' employment. But she was desperate. She got the job.

It proved harder than she had anticipated, the famous cookery writer proving tyrannical, boorish, foul-tempered, ungrateful and a remorseless slave-driver. The first week of helping him proved almost more than the young woman could stand. Only the thought of the bread she was putting in her baby's mouth prevented her from cracking.

At the end of that first purgatorial week, she was given a lift home by the cookery writer's secretary. On the way she confided how desperately she had needed this job, and how welcome would be even the paltry £400 mentioned in the advertisement.

The secretary gave her an odd look.

'I don't think you quite understand,' she said. 'It's you who've got to pay *him* £400.'

✿

An American friend was trying to put a nervous dinner-guest at ease by showing him mementoes of a recent trip to China. Among these were some tiny, exquisite carvings made from cherry-stones.

As she held the china bowl of them out for him to see, the guest gratefully scooped up two and put them into his mouth.

☆

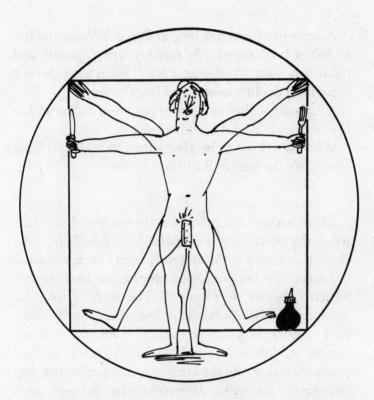

In the late Sixties, Bird's Eye brought out a variant of their ubiquitous fish fingers made from pure cod. A huge sum was committed to the new line's launch and nationwide promotion.

Only on the very eve of the launch, with TV commercials and press ads ready to roll, was the name of the product hurriedly changed from Bird's Eye Cod Pieces.

☆

A large party was lunching at Peacock Vane, the Isle of Wight hotel founded by cookery writer, painter and publisher Joan Wolfenden. Mrs Wolfenden herself brought in the first course — a large tureen.

'Chicken noodle soup,' she announced, adding in her ebullient way, 'And it's *not* Bachelor's.'

Who turned out to be giving the lunch party? None other than the head of Bachelor's Foods.

☆

There is a genre of culinary awful moment that occurs when the mistress of a household — usually in some expatriate setting — unexpectedly enters the kitchen and discovers how her employees prepare the food she has hitherto thought so exquisite. The story is told, for instance, of a British family in Malaysia whose Chinese cook was famous for producing wonderful sculpted figures of birds and animals in moist, creamy mashed potato. Straying into the kitchen unannounced one day, the lady of the house discovered what he used for a sculpting-tool.

His tongue.

While staying at Bikaner Palace, Rajasthan, in 1973, I was provided with both a butler and cook. In deference to my Englishness, the butler each morning served me with boiled eggs and toast — but the toast was always cold. I asked him to ask the cook if he could keep my toast hot while boiling my eggs. The butler promised it would be done.

Next morning, I happened to go into the kitchen while my breakfast was being prepared. My eggs were boiling away in a saucepan rigged over an open fire. Beside it sat my cook, his bare foot propped before the flames. In between each pair of toes, keeping nice and warm, was a piece of toast.

✰

It is, of course, impossible to consider awful food moments without mentioning Christmas.

I know a couple in Cambridgeshire who went out on Christmas Eve, leaving their elderly domestic to stuff the festive turkey. Unfortunately, a bottle of port also figured in the undertaking. When her employers returned, the bottle of port was empty and elderly domestic and turkey were grappling together on the kitchen floor.

At Christmas dinner, both my friends noticed that the turkey had a distinctive and not at all pleasant flavour. Their first assumption was that the plastic bag of giblets must have been left inside. The eldely domestic, however, swore that it hadn't — and even produced the empty bag as proof.

'This meat definitely tastes of plastic, though,' the master of the house insisted.

'It can't do,' his wife said. 'What else made of plastic could have got inside it?'

It was at this point that the elderly domestic clapped her hand to her mouth in horror and cried:

'My God! I've lost my teeth!'

✧

There was also the family which had the Continental habit of eating a light smoked salmon lunch, saving their appetites for the main Christmas fare at night. As the wife of the house prepared the salmon, she gave the off-cuts to the cat.

After lunch on Christmas Day, she happened to go outside and, to her horror, found the cat lying dead on the front-door mat.

Rushing inside, she babbled that the smoked salmon had been poisoned and that everyone must get medical help before they, too, succumbed. The entire family dashed to the casualty department of the nearest hospital and underwent the painful and humiliating process of being stomach-pumped.

Early that evening as they sat around, white-faced and feeling not in the least Christmassy, there was a knock at the door. The wife opened it, to find her next door neighbour.

'I'm dreadfully sorry,' he said. 'When we were on our way out today, I ran over your cat. I didn't want to disturb you at lunch, so I left it on the doormat . . .'

✧

While editing *The Sunday Times* Atticus column, I asked readers to send me accounts of the most awful Christmas they had ever spent. The winners were as follows:

'I christened it The Pregnant Turkey — and its birth pangs were shattering. It was our first Christmas bird, and my wife, overcoming her revulsion at the job of stuffing it (she wore rubber gloves and a mask and *still* averted her eyes) filled it so full that it looked as unstable as an overblown balloon. Two hours later, it exploded, flinging fragments of flesh, sage and onion through the cooker door and around the kitchen.

'My wife took one look, screamed and went to bed for the rest of the day. I, showing less restraint, karate-kicked the cooker, strained the ligaments of my big toe and lay roaring for help on the floor.

'When my passion had subsided, I clawed my way to the whisky bottle and then to the sofa. I sang carols to myself until late in the evening, when I passed out.

'I awoke to find my wife on her knees, cleaning the cooker with tears trickling down her cheeks.'

G. E. Smith

'Fiona was one of those strapping blondes in whom I find it possible to put up with a certain mental deficiency. But after dinner at her house on Christmas Eve, I realised I should have to make the same allowance for her parents. Her flatulent father clearly resented my intrusion, as did Emily the baby dachsund whose chief delight during the festivities was to tear the glass balls from the lower branches of the Christmas tree and crush them with her teeth. I felt I could take it all as I was young and in love.

'Brightly shone the moon that night, though the frost was cruel, as a young man came in sight, slipping down the passage to his beloved's door. Easing it open, whom did he find confronting him? None other than Father Christmas, aka Pater Familias, fresh from filling the beloved daughter's stocking.

'I backed down the passage on legs of tripe, mumbling something about wanting to put a present in Fiona's stocking as well. Father Christmas, with a marked scepticism of manner, suggested I might like to hang it on the tree instead.

'I had 25 yards and a short silk dressing gown in which to find a present for Fiona. In a moment of inspiration, I removed my own signet-ring. This I hung on the tree, with Father Christmas peering suspiciously over my shoulder.

'At that moment, Emily the dachsund gave a neurotic growl and fastened her jaws round my ankle. With a howl of pain, I leapt in the air, the back of my head hammering into Father Christmas's jaw, and breaking it.'

Charles P. Lucas

'My turkey and I caught the night train through Tanganyika on Christmas Eve, 1937. At dawn on Christmas Day, I was to be met at an upline station and taken to my hosts' home in the Usambara mountains.

The turkey was my contribution to the festivities. Because of the climate it, of course, had to travel live to its destination.

'Despite the rootling of the turkey in its box, I managed a few hours fitful sleep. When I awoke, it was dawn and the train was motionless next to a vast and stagnant lake. The rains had broken early, and part of the line ahead had been washed away.

'The rains cleared, and the African sun beat down on the stranded train. The stench from the turkey's box quickly became terrible. Expecting to reach my destination before breakfast, I had brought no provisions. Hot and unwashed, hungry and horribly thirsty, I spent the day staring at the turkey as it stared back at me through the wire lid of its box.

'We did not reach our destination until long after midnight. There had been no movement from the turkey in its box for several hours, and I assumed that it had expired. Gingerly, I opened the box. A furious turkey burst forth, smashed my glasses with one blow of its wing and sprinted off into the African night.'

J. J. Tawney

• • •

What is the most awful Christmas present anyone has ever received? I have two strong contenders. One is a small gilt stand, shaped like a sea-horse, for a woman to rest each finger on while painting her nails. The other —

*brought as a souvenir from the Great War battlefields —
is a miniature landmine which actually explodes,
showering the recipient with bonbons and tiny plastic
rats.*

☆

*An awful PR moment occurred earlier this year when
the first visitors toured Sellafield nuclear power station,
seeking reassurance that no lethal radiation could possibly
affect its employees or the outside world.*

The man conducting the parties round wore a wig.

☆

*One of the purported cures for baldness is to rub
castor oil into the scalp on retiring.*

*A man I know in New York gave up the treatment
after waking in the small hours and finding the top of his
head covered by feasting cockroaches.*

Print journalists are more fortunate than broadcasters in that their awful moments generally happen in relative private — before the scornful or incredulous gaze of a single interviewee — and, with any luck, can be hushed up in the subsequent copy. But then there are the awful moments brought by misprints, not to mention inapposite — or all too apposite — headlines. MOUNTING PROBLEMS FOR YOUNG COUPLES ran the heading above a story of mine in *The Cambridge Daily News*. I still wonder what quintessence of awfulness lay behind that headline some years ago in the *South China Morning Post*: WOMAN DIES OF DIARRHOEA AFTER ATTACK BY OWL.

✫

After misprints, the worst moment any journalist can experience is to file copy to his paper and then find it has not been used or else has been cut and mutilated beyond recognition. The greatest sufferers are correspondents for *Time* magazine who, each week, file yards of material from bureaux and perilous deadlines all over the world. These hard-won, expertly written dispatches from men on the spot are then collated, merged and rendered into *Time*'s own peculiar house language by desk-bound editors whose knowledge of the world is generally limited to the view outside their skyscraper window.

A few years ago, *Time* decided to run a cover story on racial tension across America. Racial tension being then particularly bad in Chicago, it was obvious that the Chicago bureau chief must play a crucial part in the operation. And indeed, spurred by numerous telephone calls and telex messages from his superiors in New York, the Chicago bureau chief rose heroically to the occasion. In the 72 hours before his deadline, he managed to interview everyone who had any relevance to racial tension in Chicago — politicians, police chiefs, Civil Rights activists. He even penetrated the notorious Blackstone ghetto and gained access to Black Power leaders never interviewed by a white journalist before. During his investigation, he was beaten up, his car was vandalised, his home and family were threatened. But he persevered and got his magnificent story.

'Send us everything,' his editors in New York commanded. In a further burst of Herculean energy, the bureau chief filed 15,000 words of poignant, gripping copy. 'It's great!' his New York editors told him. 'We may have to cut it just a *little* . . .'

Time, that week's end, devoted almost its entire issue to racial tension across America. When their Chicago bureau chief looked, the only reference to his story was one sentence: 'In Chicago the situation was much the same.'

☆

Joyce Hopkirk's career as woman's editor of the *Daily Mirror* is fondly remembered for the occasion when a male colleague informed her exasperatedly that she couldn't organise a piss-up in a brewery.

Ms Hopkirk's genial response was to book the boardroom at a leading London brewery, lay on a lavish supply of food and drink and send invitations to her accuser and other *Mirror* colleagues to attend this piss-up in a brewery she had indisputably organised.

It was a pity that all the invitations were sent bearing the wrong date.

☆

A few years ago, *The Jewish Chronicle* advertised a vacancy for a reporter with 'a good nose for a news story'.

✿

Back in the mid-Seventies, a senior executive on a Sunday newspaper was invited to take part in the BBC-TV series *One Man's Week*. A camera crew moved into the newspaper office and began assiduously filming the executive at his round of high-powered editorial conferences etc. Alas, as it soon proved, there was a problem. In common with many such eminent Fleet Street personages, the executive did virtually nothing. All the producer's ingenuity could not turn his normal working week into sufficient material for a half-hour television programme.

In despair, the producer suggested taking him back to his old college at Cambridge and filming him punting romantically down the River Cam while recalling his brilliant career as an undergraduate.

The production team moved to Cambridge, a punt was obtained and a special platform constructed on its prow to accommodate the film crew, producer and researcher. The strange-shaped craft set off, poled by the Fleet Street executive poetically dressed in white flannels.

Half-way down the river, another strangely-shaped punt came into view from the other direction. It, too, was being poled by a senior Fleet Street executive and had a platform on its prow, and a BBC camera-crew trying to get enough material for *his One Man's Week*.

✿

An elderly photographer on a north-east evening newspaper used to be given the annual job of covering the military display at Catterick Camp. The climax of the programme was a motorcycle dispatch-rider driving his machine at full speed on to a raised board, then jumping it over a line of Royal Signallers, lying prone on the grass beyond.

In all his years of shooting this daredevil feat, the elderly photographer had never managed to catch the motorcycle actually in mid-air. Somehow, he always pressed the shutter a fraction of a second too late, as the bike came down, beyond the line of recumbent soldiers.

For years, his paper had printed his boring picture of the motorcyclist riding off. But then a new Picture Editor arrived. When the Catterick display came round, the photographer was told if he didn't get the bike in mid-air this time, he'd be sacked.

He waited with extreme anxiety as the dispatch-rider roared up to the spring-board and, as the bike took off, he did at last manage to press the shutter.

Just that one year, the motorcyclist misjudged his jump and fell short, landing on the last three or four soldiers. The photographer had missed one of the picture scoops of the century.

✿

A few years ago, the photographer Tony Evans was commissioned to take a portrait of a well-known company chairman. Before the sitting, he was rung up by a rather anxious company PR lady. 'I just wanted to warn you,' she said. 'Our chairman's terribly sensitive about his big ears. Could you please not photograph him in any way that will draw attention to them? And when you meet him, please don't mention ears in any way.'

It had been arranged that Tony could call for the PR lady early in the morning and they would drive to the sitting together. As a little private joke, remembering her anxiety, Tony arrived in her street wearing a gigantic pair of rubber ears.

He rang the doorbell and waited patiently — it being still barely 7am. At last footsteps approached. As the door opened, Tony leapt into the air in his rubber ears with his arms flung wide and an expression of demented triumph.

A total stranger stared blankly out at him. He had rung the bell of the wrong house.

✿

Boxing correspondents covering the Muhammad Ali/ George Foreman fight in Kinshasa in 1974 were liberally provided with Zairoise ladies as bedfellows by the country's warm-hearted President Mobutu.

A certain American journalist joined his colleagues in the bar one morning, looking rather shaken.

He told them that during the night's frolicking with his beautiful African companion, an enormous and exotic butterfly had fluttered romantically in through the window. Whereupon his companion had reached out, grabbed it and popped it into her mouth.

✿

When I was a reporter on the *Hunts Post*, a smash and grab raid took place on the leading Huntingdon jeweller's.

The police had no difficulty in apprehending the raider. The brick he left behind in the shattered window was wrapped in a handkerchief, marked with a Cash's name-tape.

Yet another local burglar committed the common unpleasantness of defecating at the scene of the crime and leaving behind the paper with which he had wiped himself. On this happened to be written his full name and address.

✧

In 1978, I visited Blackpool to write a major magazine article on the British seaside. One of my projects was to find and interview a typical boarding-house keeper.

Early in the morning I set out, choosing a house at random. The front door was open, but no one seemed to be about. Seeing a brass gong in the front hall, I struck it loudly.

A terrible sound of downward-plodding footsteps filled the house. I had, with terrible prematureness, banged the breakfast-gong.

✧

A *Sunday Times* colleague had just handed in a complex investigative article that had taken him months to research and write and finally type into an immaculate fair copy.

Later that day, he saw his section editor reading it

desultorily in the newspaper pub over lunch. Stuck to the once flawless first page of the manuscript was a baked bean.

☆

A senior executive on a certain Sunday newspaper had the distinction of being married to an Earl's daughter. To his chagrin, however, the world sometimes seemed insufficiently aware of the fact that his wife was a 'Lady'.

Arriving with her at a diplomatic reception, he heard the major domo announce, 'Mr and Mrs — —'

He took the man aside.

'Er . . . it's not *Mrs* — —' he murmured.

'Don't worry, Sir,' the major domo replied. 'We're all broad-minded here.'

☆

Lady Kemsley's dearest wish was to be on social terms with the then King and Queen. George V, so far as is known, eluded all Her Ladyship's overtures of friendship. But in the early Thirties, after long entreaties to Buckingham Palace, half her wish, at least, was granted. Queen Mary consented to call at the Kemsley mansion for tea.

On such a private visit, clearly, coverage by the Kemsley press would be gravely inappropriate. However, Lady Kemsley was reluctant to let the occasion pass without some record of her coup. She therefore stationed a *Sunday Times* photographer in a tree whose branches overhung the main drive, with orders to take the discreetest possible picture of Queen Mary being greeted at the front door by her hostess.

The photographer, alas, was not a young man. The day was warm and, during his vigil in the tree, he nodded off to sleep. At the climactic moment when Queen Mary's limousine entered the front gate, the hapless man and his camera fell directly into its path.

Lady Kemsley, at her front door, watched the Royal conveyance carefully skirt the fallen photographer, turn in a wide arc and go out of the front gate again, for ever.

☆

The wife of Lord Kemsley was an incorrigible meddler in the running of her husband's newspapers. On one occasion, passing through the *Daily Sketch* office, she

noticed the art department laying out a picture of the supreme champion bull at that week's Smithfield Show. The reason why it was champion bull, prominently displayed in the photograph, outraged Lady Kemsley's delicate soul. She ordered that the picture be retouched, eliminating the bull's genitals.

The owner, outraged that his supreme champion should be represented as a harmless heifer, brought an action for damages against the *Daily Sketch*, and won it.

☆

During the Jordanian civil war of 1970, the entire foreign press corps found itself trapped inside Amman's unlovely Intercontinental Hotel. For three days, while rocket and tank battles raged outside, the pressmen remained under guard in the hotel's basement discotheque without food, sanitation or daylight.

As soon as they were released, they made for the checkout desk in a stampede. Each of their bills, they found, bore the usual 15 per cent service charge.

☆

When Harold Wilson effected a drastic reshuffle of his Labour Cabinet in 1969, the London *Evening Standard*'s front-page banner headline — hurriedly changed in later editions — read:

OUT COMES THE WILSON CHOPPER

☆

L. Marsland Gander, the *Daily Telegraph*'s veteran TV critic, wrote his own obituary notice for the paper. On submitting an invoice to the accounts department, he was told that payment would be on publication.

☆

In 1967, as a young, inexperienced writer for *The Sunday Times* Magazine, I was sent to Salzburg to interview Elizabeth Taylor. She was extremely kind, allowing me to watch her on her film set and afterwards drive back to her hotel with her, and her two Pekinese dogs, in the back of an immense Cadillac.

I have suffered from car sickness since childhood and,

in the overheated limo' amid a swirl of exotic scents from the star and her Pekes, I felt the old, terrible symptoms coming on. My only hope, I knew from long experience, was to look at the road straight ahead. Meanwhile, I had to continue interviewing Elizabeth Taylor.

'Please don't think I'm not paying attention,' I told her. 'But if I look at you, I shall feel sick.'

✡

A colour supplement journalist recently went down to Buckinghamshire to interview that wild red-haired polemicist Paul Johnson. During their conversation, Johnson said he hoped the writer would join his wife and himself for lunch. 'When your photographer gets here,' he added, 'I've arranged for him to have lunch down at the pub.'

Just then the 'photographer' arrived. It was Lord Snowdon.

• • •

He was the epitome of the City stockbroker one sees on the Underground in rush hour, immaculate and very irritable, reading a Financial Times *which, from time to time, he would snap aside to scowl with withering scorn at the lesser mortals around him.*

He sat there for stop after stop, alternately reading and scowling, blissfully unaware that, stuck to the outside of his paper, low down where he could not see it, was a piece of toast and marmalade.

☆

During the North African campaign in the Second World War, a party of British sappers were deep in the Libyan desert, clearing Rommel's diabolically-clever anti-tank mines.

As they ate their midday meal, a Stuka dive bomber came screaming out of the sky. The sappers leapt for the shallow fox-holes they had dug. One man, in his panic, chose a fox-hole already full of bodies, and found himself still in view of the Stuka without even a tin hat to protect him. As a reflex he grabbed the nearest tin meal plate and clapped it on to his head.

It happened, at the time, to be full of warm rice pudding.

☆

St Chad's Cathedral, Birmingham, recently joined the many sacred edifices now fitted with 'halter' microphones, so that every detail of services may be heard by even the most distant worshippers.

Shortly afterwards, a ceremony took place there, at which Archbishop George Patrick O'Dwyer was attended by a young and nervous chaplain. At the conclusion of the ceremony, the chaplain approached the enthroned archbishop with the mitre and ceremonially placed it on his head.

To his horror, he saw that he's put it on back to front: the finials were falling over the archbishop's eyes. He stepped forward again hastily and attempted to rotate the mitre to its proper angle.

Over the sound-system, into the furthest parts of the cathedral, a peevish voice protested 'There's no need to screw *the bloody thing on.*'

She was one of these luckless little New York girls whose anorexically thin mothers still allow them to swell up into popcorn-fed obesity. I felt for her even before I heard a friend of her mother exclaim 'Oh, she's . . .' and then pause for a fatal half-second. 'Oh, she's got such a pretty *face*.'

Do you remember, as I do, moments in childhood when such a stray remark from the grown-up world took one to the very bottom of the abyss of despair, and nobody noticed?

Do you remember going into rooms full of grown-ups, longing for nothing more than to be treated as an equal by them, and to stand there, sipping little drinks and being sophisticated? Do you remember the heart-shrivelling remarks with which your parents exposed your pitiful childish station. They would ask, with a ghastly semblance of kindness, if you wanted another fizzy lemonade, or whether you wouldn't be happier out in the garden 'playing with the doggies'.

When you took your first girl or boyfriend home, do you remember that inner tension, as of entering a canyon where every rock might conceal a sharpshooting Apache? Even if your mother did not regale the beloved one with details of your early toilet training, you knew you could not yet relax. For your father still had to come in and meet the beloved one and, possibly say — in a voice freighted with the knowing irony that made you want to jump from the nearest 20-storey window — 'Ah . . . so *this* is Cynthia!'

Parents never lost their ability to mortify their children

to the bone, as the mother of a friend of mine proved, even on her wedding day. 'Well — you're no beauty dear,' her mother told her, 'but the dress *is* lovely.'

☆

My old school classmate Peter Read had been invited home to meet the parents of his first girlfriend.

During tea, the loved one's mother asked politely about the private school which he (and I) attended. Peter strove for the grown-up note in conveying his low opinion of its teaching.

'Most of the staff are very bad at keeping order,' he said. 'The boys spend nearly all their time master-baiting.'

☆

Georgina Howell's father remembered a master at Bedford School whose passion for mountaineering could unfailingly be exploited by his class to provide a respite from ordinary lessons. One day, skilfully sidetracked from Latin or Scripture, he was beguiled into explaining the technique for ascending a sheer rock-face, using the thickly-stuccoed classroom-wall as an illustration.

'Sir, does that mean you could climb this wall?' his class enquired.

'Certainly — if I did it the proper way.'

'Oh Sir, Sir,' the crafty boys clamoured. '*Please* show us!'

So the enthusiastic master began to scale the wall, using the stucco for hand and foot holds, giving a commentary over his shoulder to his ecstatic class.

He had reached a point well above the classroom door when it suddenly opened and the headmaster walked in.

✩

In the Sixth Form at school, I did English with a headmaster brilliant at his subject but a stern disciplin-arian. The fact that there were only three of us on the A Level course still brooked no lapses in decorum — and, especially, no giggling or smut.

Occasionally, however, free discussion on literary topics was allowed. One morning, the head invited our opinions about the suitability of Dickens' books to be turned into cinema films.

I said I thought that *Oliver Twist* was one of the best films ever made. Gerald Littler, on my right at the Library table, said he thought the same about *Great Expectations*.

From the other side of the table, the future Reverend Peter Miln spoke in a boom that, even then, seemed to belong to the pulpit.

'I see,' he remarked, 'that they've started to film The Sale of Two Titties.' *

* A surpassingly awful grown-up version of this happened when I was interviewing Indira Gandhi in 1972. Towards the end, I asked the aloof and unsmiling Prime Minister which of her advisers I might talk to for background on the current Indian political situation.

Turning her frosty eyes upon me, Mrs Gandhi replied, 'I think the best person you could speak to would be Mr Dickshit.'

104

✿

One of my old colleagues at *The Sunday Times* was out for a walk recently when a small boy approached him, looking disconsolate and pushing a bicycle. My friend asked him what was wrong. He replied that his bicycle-chain had come adrift. My kind-hearted friend took the bicycle from him, knelt down and replaced the chain. Then — liberally daubed in oil and spirit — he explained how the chain could be reset and the tension adjusted if it came off again.

'Oh . . . I know how to do it,' the stripling replied. 'It's just that doing it always makes my hands so dirty.'

✿

A companion of my senior school days was inhibited in most of his adolescent desires by an extremely powerful and punctilious mother. One day, he came to school in great excitement to say that his mother would be going away that next weekend, and he intended to throw the party of a lifetime.

It was certainly that. Indeed, the first thing his mother beheld, on returning home the next Monday morning, was a used Durex lying on the front doorstep.

Terrible ructions ensued. For the rest of that day, the guilty son took flak and laboured to make amends with grovelling apologies, flowers, chocolates and promises on his honour that such a dreadful, disgusting thing would never *ever* happen again. By evening, he was exhausted — and just about forgiven.

His mother retired to bed and turned back the counterpane. Nestling in the centre of her pillow was another used Durex.

✧

A schoolfriend of Russell Miller borrowed his father's cherished car for his first essay in teenage lovemaking. Afterwards, he carefully swept the interior clean of all traces of what had occurred.

Next morning, watching his father majestically drive off to work, he saw that the Durex he'd thrown out of the window last night was clinging to the rear passenger-door.

✧

A boy at my school took his motor scooter test in Newport, IOW, a town of twisty streets and sudden corners.

For most of the test, his examiner rode behind him on the pillion-seat, not dismounting until the very last. 'Now,' the examiner said. 'I want you to ride once round the block. When you come back, I shall test you on an emergency stop by stepping out in front of you.'

My friend obediently rode round the block, but found himself delayed by a whole series of traffic-jams and red lights. When he returned at last, he saw his examiner being put into an ambulance. A few minutes earlier, *another* scooter had come round the corner, and the examiner had stepped out in front of it.

✿

Tony Evans lost his hair at an early age, but did not let this inhibit his courtship of young ladies. On the contrary, he traded on it. To amuse a young shop assistant he admired, he walked into her shop one day with an adhesive joke zip-fastener on the top of his head.

Only at the end of that day, after several rather serious subsequent appointments, did he realise he'd forgotten to take it off.

✿

The friend of a friend recently awoke in a strange bed in South Kensington, next to the Sloane Ranger with whom he had drunkenly spent the night. Try as he might, he could not remember where they had met or what had later transpired. He could not even remember the sleeping girl's name.

The only way to find out before she awoke seemed to be to look in her driving-licence. He therefore slipped out of bed, found her handbag, opened her wallet and began to rummage in it.

Unluckily she chose that very moment to open her eyes.

✿

An Isle of Wight Hell's Angel met a specially awful end a few years ago, on one of the island's narrow roads.

It was late at night. Coming up behind two wide-apart red tail lights, the Hell's Angel assumed they belonged to

two cyclists, and thought what fun it would be to roar
through in between them.

The tail-lights, of course, belonged to a heavy lorry.

☆

Posy Simmonds remembers the occasion in her teenage
years when she first went out with back-combed hair,

stiffened into shape, as such beehives used to be, with a solution of sugar and water.

The day was hot, the sugar melted and before she knew it, her whole bouffant was a mass of buzzing flies.

✧

When John Betjeman became engaged to his future wife Penelope, her exceedingly grand father called the young poet aside and said that from now on it would not be necessary for Betjeman to address him as 'Sir'.

Henceforward, just 'Field Marshal' would be sufficient.

● ● ●

Awful moments suffered by deliverers of singing telegrams are probably no more than their due. Still, my heart goes out to the girl, en route to deliver a singing telegram in a gorilla-suit, who accidentally drove her car into the middle of the Iranian Embassy siege.

✧

A female acquaintance whose husband had left her for another woman decided she would not, after all, let the divorce go through without some unequivocal statement of her feelings.

She resolved to go to the house where husband and girlfriend had already set up together, and throw a brick through the window of their sitting-room.

She did so — and was surprised, on meeting her

husband a few days afterwards, that he showed no signs whatever of anger or resentment.

'We don't know if we like our new street after all,' he remarked conversationally. 'We were sitting downstairs after dinner the other night, and some lunatic came and threw a brick through the window of the house next door.'

✳

A spectacularly imaginative awful moment was devised by a young woman who had discovered her boy friend to be week-ending abroad with Someone Else.

Gaining admittance to his very expensive and tastefully furnished flat, she turned up the central heating, poured water over the carpets, sofas and armchairs, then sprinkled them liberally with mustard and cress seed.

When the errant boy friend returned home, he found every surface thick with mustard and cress, doing beautifully.

Not long ago I heard that doyen of travel writers Eric Newby recalling the trip he made with his wife in an open boat down the River Ganges.

'My wife was suffering from dysentery rather badly. And, of course, being in an open dug-out, there was absolutely no privacy. It got so bad that even our Indian boatman deserted us. And then, just a few moments later, we were attacked by a tribe of baboons.'

I have nothing but admiration for professional travellers and the valour with which, time and again, they go forth to meet the unpredictable worst that can be done by foreign airports, cities, jungles, deserts, oceans, swamps and diplomatic receptions. My own travels for *The Sunday Times* I tend to regard as something that, by an all-protecting mixture of ignorance and naïveté, I just about got away with. I just got away with interviewing Colonel Gaddafi, with being held at gunpoint alongside Richard Burton in Salzburg, and with an assault on my virtue by a 6ft 6in Jordanian test pilot (an awful moment which I still do not feel quite up to recounting).

As I write these entries, I think more and more that I shall probably never again venture east of Harwich.

✠

A young couple on an adventure holiday in Chad had armed themselves with every form of protection against disease, including a course of anti-malaria tablets which they took each morning at breakfast.

One morning, having swallowed the tablets, both began to froth violently at the mouth.

The husband had mixed up the malaria pills with the effervescent water-purifying tablets.

✧

An English friend living in New York had bought a second-hand television set, and resolved to carry it home by subway, even though he lived right Downtown and the hour was getting late.

As he stood on the empty platform holding the TV set, a vast black man sauntered up and, in a voice heavy with menace, said 'Hey man, gimme a quarter.'

Balancing the TV set on one knee, my friend groped in his trouser-pocket, extracted a dollar bill and handed it over. The black man sauntered off.

My friend, certain he would soon be back, clung to the TV set, praying for the train to come, and resolutely not looking along the platform.

As the train lights approached, a heavy hand tapped him on the shoulder. He turned, fearing the worst.

'Hey,' the black man said. 'Here's your change.'

✧

A party of British businessmen were visiting Moscow in the late Fifties — that era when all westerners in Russia believed the KGB to be bugging them 24 hours a day.

At a loose end one evening, the businessmen decided to find the bug in one of their hotel rooms. They ransacked the room — even finally rolling back the carpet. There in the centre of the floor was a raised

113

metal stud, held in place by six screws. So *that* was how the KGB did it!

Amid general triumph, one of the businessmen produced a screwdriver and began to take out the screws.

As he lifted the 'bug' from the floor, a muffled crash came from directly underneath.

It was a chandelier falling into the hotel's main banquet-hall.

✧

While lecturing on journalism in West Germany, my old colleague Don Berry decided to make use of the very luxurious local swimming baths.

As with all in West Germany, getting into the baths involved several highly bureaucratic stages. At last, having passed through all the checkpoints for payment, acquiring a locker-key, getting in and out of the changing-room and acquiring a towel, he arrived at the poolside. Only then did he realise to his dismay that, while he was respectably attired in swimming trunks, everyone else in the water was naked.

Unable to go backwards through the checkpoints, he had no option but to swim in his trunks, feeling extremely silly and uncomfortable.

Next day, he decided to visit the baths again. He knew what he must do — and, to help his resolve, left his swimming-trunks behind at the hotel.

It was only after going through all the checkpoints and arriving at the poolside stark naked that he realised everyone else in the water wore costumes.

114

✿

In the days when Paris was oh-so-naughty, a middle-aged Isle of Wight couple went there for the weekend.

On the first morning, while the wife shopped, the husband determined to try his luck with a lasy of pleasure.

Catching the eye of a girl in the Place Pigalle, he approached her and furtively enquired how much she charged.

'Five thousan' francs' was the reply.

'But . . . I've only got five hundred,' he said.

'Pah! Impossible!' the girl retorted, tossing her head and walking on.

Later, having had no luck, the husband rejoined his wife. As they strolled along the Champs Elysée, they suddenly came face to face with the girl he had accosted.

'Zere you are!' she exclaimed, pointing scornfully at the wife. 'You see what you get for five 'undred francs!'

✿

Russell Miller, on a pleasure cruise to the Bahamas, hurriedly changed his restaurant table after the conversational opening gambit of the American woman seated next to him:

'We almost didn't come on this cruise. A week ago, my husband came to me and said "Myra — I think my stomach's going wrong. My stools have turned black again."'

✿

In the mid-Fifties when Michaela Denis was the queen of African safari programmes, she visited the wife of an obscure game warden, Joy Adamson, who had begun to hand-rear a lioness named Elsa. Their story ultimately became the globally best-selling book and movie, *Born Free*.

At this earlier time, the unknown Joy Adamson gave the famous Michaela Denis some rough film footage of Elsa, asking her to try to interest someone in London in it. The footage, somehow or other, found its way into the Denis's *On Safari* programme, adding lustre to their name rather than Joy Adamson's.

When Michaela next visited the Adamsons on their African reserve, she took with her the young David Attenborough. Joy was waiting — and wasted no time in verbal reproaches. As Michaela got out of the Land Rover, an enraged female figure in bush clothes sprang on her like the lioness in question. Attenborough watched in amazement as the two first women of Africa rolled, spitting and snarling, in the dust.

✧

The remarkable journey made by Quentin Crewe in his wheelchair across the desert, accompanied by a *Weekend Telegraph* reporter and an Arab guide, included a moment not found in the subsequent article.

At one point, supplies began to run low. The Arab guide came to the photographer and with Bedouin logic said things would be far easier if they could abandon the man in the wheelchair.

116

✡

Some years ago, a death occurred among the passengers on a cruise ship in the Indian Ocean. Since the vessel was more than a week away from her next port-of-call, there was no alternative but to hold a burial at sea.

By long maritime tradition, the practical arrangements for burials at sea devolve on the ship's bosun. He it is who provides the Union Jack in which the body is wrapped and the plank on which it is tipped overboard. By equally long tradition, these duties are recompensed by an extra ration of grog.

The extra ration of grog played its part when, testing the plank at the ship's rail on the day before the burial, the bosun suddenly felt unsure if it was well-polished enough for the corpse to slide smoothly along it. His assistant — who had shared the double ration of grog — suggested there was only one way to find out. Accordingly, they went below, fetched the passenger's corpse from the deep freeze, carried it on deck and placed it on the plank, to see whether it would slide smoothly just a little way.

Unfortunately, when they tilted the plank, neither was holding the corpse tightly enough. To their horror, it whizzed off the end and into the sea.

Clearly, neither the grieving relatives nor the ship's captain could be told that the burial had taken place 24 hours early. So, with a true seafarers' ingenuity, the bosun and his mate went to the galley and got about 100 large, knobbly potatoes. These they sewed into the Union Jack. The result was so utterly corpse-like, they were certain no one at the real funeral could possibly know the difference.

Next day, the sad ceremony was held. The Captain spoke the prayer and, at the words 'We now commit his body to the deep . . .' gave the signal to the bosun to tilt the plank.

Unfortunately, the unnatural weight tilted the plank sideways, the 'corpse' fell off, on to the deck, the stitches on its shroud parted, and King Edward potatoes went noisily bouncing everywhere.

✧

A strong contender for the most awful moment in a bathroom abroad is supplied by Peter Gillman.

Visiting Patagonia in the early Seventies, he called on an English expatriate there, a naturalist whose house was crammed with strange and exotic things collected on his travels. Gillman, even so, was hardly prepared for what he found when he went to pee.

Lying in the bath was a dead penguin.

✧

The naturalist's only companion, Gillman goes on, was a tiny kitten, which frisked charmingly around the two men as they talked.

Gillman then left to go on a journey to Terra del Fuego. On his return a fortnight later, he visited the naturalist again. As they talked this time, he noticed there was no little kitten frisking around.

'Have you lost your kitten?' he asked.

'No,' the naturalist said. 'He died, just a couple of days after you were here.'

118

'Oh — I'm sorry,' Gillman sympathised.

'Mm, he was a nice little chap wasn't he?' the naturalist said absently, pointing to the kitten's corpse lying on top of a nearby wastepaper basket.

☆

A British art director, staying at New York's Helmsley Palace Hotel, had spent a riotous evening with some American colleagues. Returning to his room in a highly tired and emotional state, he collapsed on to the counter-pane of his freshly turned-down king-size bed and fell into a deep sleep. Awakening, fully clothed, in the small hours, he became conscious of a reeking stickiness all over his face. He had forgotten the American hotel custom of leaving large chocolate mints on each guest's pillow last thing at night.

☆

Two female *Sunday Times* colleagues, strolling along Bombay seafront, paused at a display of attractive-looking knitwear, spread out on a sloping counter. Each of my colleagues saw several things she fancied, and asked the Indian in charge if they could try them on. 'Certainly, ladies,' the Indian replied, handing the items over.

They both spent several minutes in trying things on, and chose several sweaters and cardigans each. 'We'd like all these,' they told the Indian in charge. 'How much are they?'

He smiled a delighted smile.

'Oh ladies . . .' he said. 'This is a laundry.'

Colin Jones's worst moment as an international photographer was waking up in a road house in Zaire and seeing a crowd of gigantic cockroaches carrying off his socks.

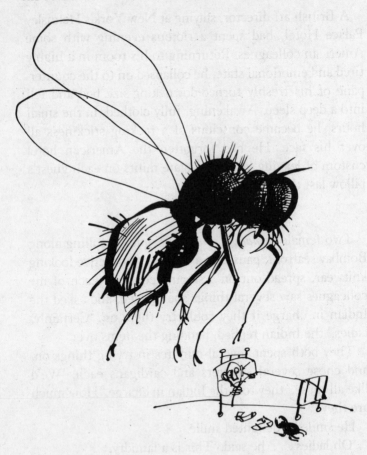

✧

A lady from Dublin had spent years saving up for a trip to Lourdes to witness that poignant annual ceremony when the physically handicapped come hoping to be healed at the Shrine of St Bernadette.

The lady from Dublin was so moved and excited to be in Lourdes at last, she got up at dawn on the appointed day and reached the shrine several hours before the ceremony was due to begin. As time went on, the sun grew hot and she started to feel a little faint. There was nowhere to sit, but in one of a line of empty wheelchairs awaiting the pilgrimage down into the healing grotto.

The lady from Dublin therefore sat down in a wheelchair and, what with heat and over-excitement, nodded off to sleep.

When she awoke, the wheelchair was moving. While asleep, she had been added to the procession of the handicapped, now fully underway and moving towards the Shrine of St Bernadette, watched by large and emotional crowds of sympathisers.

In high alarm, the lady from Dublin sprang out of the wheelchair. Those standing near saw her and began to cry 'Our Lady be praised! It's a miracle!'

Unfortunately, the man pushing the wheelchair did not stop in time, and pushed it on into the lady from Dublin, knocking her over and breaking her leg.

She is perhaps the only person ever to have returned from Lourdes more afflicted than when she went.

PIECES OF HATE

A treasury of invective and abuse

Philip Norman

Illustrated by Paula Youens

I dedicate this collection to those who, like me, are apt to go a bit too far. Which, as we know, is usually just far enough.

If you haven't got a good word to say about anyone, come and sit near me – Emerald Cunard

PIECES OF HATE

Among the civic bodies that aroused President L. B. Johnson's Southern ire was one called The Association of American States.

'The Association of American States', said LBJ, 'couldn't pour piss out of a shoe if the instructions were written on the heel.'

A *Daily Express* executive received a summons from Lord Beaverbrook while snatching a few minutes respite on the lavatory.

'Tell Lord Beaverbrook,' the man replied to his boss's emissary through the cubicle-door, 'that I can only deal with one shit at a time.'

A television critic in 1979 described Bruce Forsyth as 'Uriah Heep on speed'.

A friend's epitaph to W. H. Auden:

'I don't think you could say Wystan loved God exactly. Fancied Him, perhaps . . .'

127

Journalists involved in Rupert Murdoch's *Sunday Times* takeover and his subsequent exodus to Wapping were heard to complain they were treated rather like mushrooms.

They were kept completely in the dark, and every now and then their employer came along and poured shit on them.

Coral Browne is credited with the saltiest tongue in the theatre.

A few years ago, at a Hollywood party, she fell into conversation with a young director who praised her performance in her newest film, but said he thought the script was not well-written. Alas, he did not know that the writer was a close friend of Ms Browne's.

'Don't talk to me about writing,' she advised him. '*You* couldn't write "fuck" on a dusty Venetian blind.'

It was widely said of the late Peggy Guggenheim that she didn't have a nose — she had an eggplant.

At a publishing party recently, two editors watched as the great Naim Atallah passed by, his few grey strands of hair as usual carefully flattened across his skull.

'How would you describe that hair?' one editor mused.

The other reflected and answered, 'Like an appendectomy scar.'

As Ruby Wax said of TV's diminutive sex therapist Dr Ruth:

'Who wants to talk about making it with someone who looks like a squashed chihuahua?'

Four glamorous faces on the side of a London bus looked strangely familiar to the mother of a teenage acquaintance.

'Isn't that Bucks Fizz?' she said. 'Didn't they have a bad car accident a little while ago?'

'Not bad enough,' her son replied.

A commentator on the 1987 election observed that Neil Kinnock, at moments of high oratorial passion, looked like nothing so much as a tortoise having an orgasm.

Watching Richard Branson ditch in the sea at the end of his recent Atlantic crossing, a friend commented:

'That's what always happens when you put a prick too near a balloon.'

Reporting the wedding of Prince Charles in 1981, Clive James noted that the thickness of mascara around Barbara Cartland's eyes made them resemble 'a couple of small crows which had fatally crashed into a chalk cliff.'

American columnist William F. Buckley was asked if he anticipated any difficulty in an approaching TV interview with Senator Edward Kennedy.

He replied 'Does baloney resist the grinder?'

For wicked epitaphs, one could hardly beat what an executive at RCA Records said on being told of Elvis Presley's death:

'Good career move.'

In Liverpool, footballers are encouraged to more aggressive tackling by the cry, 'Tear 'is leg off and 'it 'im with the soggy end.'

George Orwell wrote that the members of the Aesthetic Movement between the wars 'spent on sodomy what they got by sponging.'

Randolph Churchill once had to go into hospital for investigation of a tumour, which was subsequently pronounced not malignant.

Evelyn Waugh remarked how brilliant it had been of medical science 'to find the one part of Randolph that is not malignant.'

Old saying: How can you tell when a politician is lying? His lips move.

Contemplating the awesome costs of his doomed film epic *Raise the Titanic*, Sir Lew Grade was heard to murmur gloomily that it would have been cheaper to lower the Atlantic.

After Chappaquiddick, it was said around Washington that the only person in the world now likely to accept a lift home from Edward Kennedy was Jacques Cousteau.

A coldly hostile conversation between two journalistic colleagues ended with the following exchange:

First colleague: 'Right — I'll make a mental note of that.'

Second colleague: 'On what?'

Esther Rantzen was recently bitten by a tame polecat during rehearsals for one of her wacky 'That's Life' items.

The Sun's *headline next day was:*

   POLECAT BITES ESTHER RANTZEN AND LIVES

Jayne Mansfield used to define a man as a creature with two legs and eight hands.

The nickname of a specially devious and pusillanimous London magazine editor is Hello, He Lied.

At a society wedding in the Thirties, Tallulah Bankhead sniffed disparagingly as the bride and groom passed.

'I've had them both,' she said. 'And they were *both* lousy.'

Sir Laurence Olivier's extravagantly ethnic performance as Othello was known for short in the theatrical world as 'Hello, Golly'.

The Jordanian newspaper *El Shri* recently said in an editorial that Nancy Reagan's smile 'is the best argument we in the Muslim world have seen for the reinstitution of the veil.'

Peter Cook once dubbed David Frost 'The Bubonic Plagiarist.'

Lorenz Hart, composer of such matchless boy-girl love songs as 'Bewitched, Bothered and Bewildered', was in fact a homosexual, sometimes known for short among Broadway colleagues as 'Bitched, Buggered and Bedildoed'.

During the Second World War, Anthony Eden sent Churchill a memorandum of dullness exceptional even for him. It came back with a single comment by Churchill, scrawled in the margin.

'This document seems to contain every cliché excepting "God is love" and "Please adjust your dress before leaving".'

Northern comedian to heckler:

'Why don't you go and play among the traffic.'

The Today newspaper is known throughout Fleet Street as 'The Technicolour Yawn'.

One of our livelier feminists has observed that God invented Man because a vibrator couldn't mow the lawn.

135

W. S. Gilbert once received an angry note from his neighbour Mr Crosse — of Crosse & Blackwell foods — to the effect that he'd been unlawfully shooting Crosse's pheasants.

'Tell Mr Crosse,' Gilbert instructed a secretary, 'that I would not *dream* of touching his preserves.'

In Liverpool, a person of small stature is said to be 'built like a racing tadpole.'

On tour with the Rolling Stones in 1972, Truman Capote observed that Mick Jagger was 'about as sexy as a pissing toad.'

Dean Martin's fondness for 'the sauce' has led to innumerable wisecracks from his Hollywood contemporaries.

Red Buttons, a few years ago, said that if Dracula bit Dean in the neck, he'd get a Bloody Mary.

Buttons added that Dean had recently undergone a difficult surgical operation — to have a brass rail removed from under his foot.

Variety once headlined the obituary of a Hollywood producer:
INFLUENCE GREAT BUT NEVER HAD A HIT.

A Liberal opponent remarked last year that giving the National Health Service into Mrs Thatcher's charge was 'like putting Doctor Mengele on the board of Mothercare.'

When Shaw and Churchill traded verbal crotch-kicks, the result was generally a draw.

In the early Thirties, Shaw invited Churchill to one of his first nights, enclosing two tickets 'so that you can bring a friend . . . if you have one.'

Churchill wrote back, saying he was afraid he couldn't be at the first night but would be delighted to attend the second . . . 'if there is one.'

Clive James said in 1979 that a typical speech by Margaret Thatcher 'sounds like the Book of Revelations read over a railway station public address system by a headmistress of a certain age wearing calico knickers.'

Told of the death of a certain Hollywood actress, Robert Benchley produced this simple epitaph:

'She sleeps alone at last.'

Shaw was the earliest anti-smoking campaigner. Those who resist nicotine pollution still quote his exchange with an ostentatiously liberated Edwardian woman one day on the Great Western Railway.

'I hope you won't mind if I smoke,' the woman said brightly.

'Certainly not,' Shaw answered. 'And I hope you won't mind if I'm sick.'

The woman bridled angrily.

'I'll have you know', she said, 'that I'm one of the directors' wives.'

'Madam,' Shaw said, 'if you were the director's *only* wife I should still be sick.'

John Cole on rising Tory minister Kenneth Clarke:
  'I have seen the future, and it smirks.'

The Marquess of Queensberry's attempts to provoke Oscar Wilde included presenting him publicly with a crude bouquet of garden vegetables.

'Thank you, Lord Queensberry,' Wilde replied. 'Whenever I look at them I shall think of you.'

BEST CAULIFLOWER

On the day Mrs Thatcher signed the Channel Tunnel agreement in Canterbury Cathedral's Chapter House, a local clergyman was asked for his view by BBC radio.

'One can only think,' he replied 'of what Christ did with the moneychangers in the Temple.'

'Was that quite the same?' the radio reporter demurred.

'Not quite,' the feisty clergyman agreed. 'Christ threw the moneychangers straight into the street. He didn't let them stop off in the Chapter House and ruin the economy.'

When literary critic of the *New Yorker*, Dorothy Parker wrote of a certain novel that it was 'not a book to be lightly tossed aside . . . but thrown with great force.'

After making *The Incredible Shrinking Woman*, Lily Tomlin appeared on the Dick Cavett late-night talk show.

'Tell me, Lily,' Cavett said mockingly. 'What's the advantage in being an incredible shrinking woman?'

'Well firstly, Dick, it lets me talk to people like you,' Ms Tomlin replied.

Evelyn Waugh wrote of Stephen Spender that one watched him use the English language 'with the same horrified fascination as watching a Sèvres vase in the hands of a chimpanzee.'

A profile of Yoko Ono in The Village Voice *a few years ago bore the headline:*

JOHN RENNON'S GLOOPIE

When Margaret Thatcher became Prime Minister, Germaine Greer wrote that Britain was now ruled by a woman who couldn't tell a joke and governed by a woman who couldn't understand one.

During the Wapping print dispute, Rupert Murdoch's embattled plant, with its hapless journalistic internees, became known round Fleet Street as 'The Lost City of the Inkies'.

⁓

Truman Capote said of a certain notable New York society hostess that kissing her was 'like playing Postman's Knock with a dead whale.'

⁓

Screenwriter Larry Gelbart was asked what lesson he had learned from working with the multi-talented but temperamental Dustin Hoffman.

'It taught me,' Gelbart said, 'never to work with any actor smaller than his Oscar.'

⁓

Max Beerbohm hit on the perfect double-edged gush, invited backstage by a great Edwardian actress after seeing her give a performance of monumental dullness.

'Darling!' Max exclaimed, opening his arms. 'Good was *not* the word!'

143

In the 18th century, few possessed the ruthless wit of the insurrectionary John Wilkes.

'Mr Wilkes,' the Earl of Sandwich once said to him, 'I do not know whether you will be hanged or die of the pox.'

Wilkes replied, 'That depends, My Lord, whether I embrace your political principles or your mistress.'

Janet Street-Porter recently described Samantha Fox in a leather suit as having looked like 'a badly-wrapped black pudding'.

On Harold Macmillan's ruthless Cabinet purge of 1963, Jeremy Thorpe commented, 'Greater love hath no man than he who lays down his friends for his life.'

One of John Osborne's former wives remembers the great kitchen sink dramatist shrieking at her, 'I'm sick of all your mute attrition!'

An old Irish malediction runs:
'May you marry a ghost, may it bear you a kitten, and may the Good Lord give it the mange.'

'After being struck on the head by her husband Sean Penn, Madonna was rushed to hospital for a brain-scan. But nothing was found.'

— *Capital Radio*

At the *Sunday Times Magazine*'s 25th anniversary party, Frankie Howerd asked Russell Harty if he had been away on holiday yet and, on being told that he hadn't, inquired, 'Have you considered Lourdes?'

After the recent television profile of designer Michael Roberts, a friend commented that it had revealed all his hidden shallows.

When Gerald Ford assumed the American Presidency, his intellectual powers were summed up by a widespread belief that he couldn't walk and scratch his arse at the same time.

Hamlet has been summarised by a non-admirer as:
>A play in which a ghost and a prince meet
>And nearly everyone ends up mincemeat

145

On meeting his betrothed, Princess Caroline of Brunswick, the Prince Regent's only recorded words were: 'Harris, I am not well. Get me a glass of brandy.'

One reviewer of Bernard Levin's recent book *Enthusiasms* said that its author wrote 'like an elephant with a wet mouth.'

Another reviewer compared the effect of Levin's prose to 'farting through trumpets.'

NBC TV's movie critic ended his scathing review of the sci-fi epic *Dune* by suggesting its makers had got the last letter of the title wrong. It should have been a 'g'.

Marianne Faithfull was telling a friend at the Chelsea Arts Club that she'd just been on a visit to Berlin.

'Berlin! How appropriate,' the friend replied. 'Armies have passed through you both.'

Cricketer Phil Edmonds's wife says how much simpler his life on tour has become since he does not have to bother packing shampoo or hair-conditioner. 'All he needs these days is a duster and a squirt of Pledge.'

The Gault-Millau restaurant guide to New York reports that Elaine, of Elaine's, has a smile 'with all the charm of a slammed door.'

Macaulay described Byron's poetry as 'a system of ethics with two great commandments — hate thy neighbour and love thy neighbour's wife.'

A colleague on Louis B. Mayer:

'If you're LB's enemy, he destroys you. If you're his friend, he eats you.'

A few years ago, *Private Eye* published a story about a businessman named Mr Arkell. It brought a solicitor's letter in the usual loftily threatening form . . . 'our client takes a grave view of this defamatory statement . . . requires a retraction to be printed prominently in your next issue . . . our attitude to damages and costs will be governed by the nature of your reply.'

Private Eye's editor replied:

'Dear Sirs, we thank you for your letter on behalf of Mr Arkell. We note that your attitude to damages and costs will be governed by the nature of our reply, and should be interested to know what that attitude will be on discovering that the nature of our reply is as follows — Fuck off.'

Of that taxing and puzzling play The Ice Man Cometh, Observer *critic C. A. Lejeune merely wrote 'It is longeth and it stinketh.'*

The caustic courtroom wit of Edward Carson, KC, did not draw the line even at judges.

'Mr Carson,' a testy judge interrupted as he was cross-examining. 'Why is it that everything you say is going in one of my ears and out the other?'

'Nothing to stop it, me lud,' Carson replied.

'Do you drink?' he once asked a bewhiskered Victorian in the witness box.

'That's my business,' the witness replied brusquely.

'Any other business?' Carson inquired.

Eve Arnold remembers asking her brother in New York if he'd been seeing much of his somewhat formidable mother-in-law.

'The last time I saw her,' he replied, 'she was climbing up the Empire State Building with King Kong in her mouth.'

Speaking at a dinner recently, Tommy Docherty mentioned how sorry he was that a rival football manager had been unable to attend the event, through illness.

'When he woke up this morning, I'm told he was covered in love bites . . . all self-inflicted, of course.'

A rising young Fleet Street executive is known among colleagues as 'The Eminence Grease'.

Dorothy Parker was famous among her *New Yorker* colleagues for suicide attempts that were clearly designed to be foiled.

When news of yet another overdose and dramatic rescue reached the *New Yorker*, Alexander Woolcott commented, 'If Dottie isn't careful she's going to hurt herself one of these days.'

Margot Asquith used to say that a day away from Tallulah Bankhead was like a month in the country.

Randolph Churchill was notorious for wrecking dinner parties with his outbursts of rage and furious exits.

In the mortified silence following one such exit, Noel Coward was heard to murmur 'Dear Randolph . . . quite unspoiled by failure.'

It is said of Sir Geoffrey Howe that he can brighten up a room just by leaving it.

Edward VII's habit of taking yacht trips with tea millionaire Sir Thomas Lipton led Kaiser Wilhelm II to remark disparagingly one day that his Royal uncle was 'out boating with his grocer.'

In the Sixties, Sir John Gielgud appeared in a production of *Oedipus Rex* whose stage set consisted entirely of cubes in various sizes, which the cast either stood on or crouched inside.

'I know what we should really call this,' Sir John remarked sotto voce at one point, '*Cocks and Box*'.

During his hapless efforts to get Peter Wright's spy memoirs banned in Australia, Cabinet Secretary Sir Robert Armstrong was dubbed by the Press 'a wally among the wallabies.'

A schoolfriend of mine — a lah-de-dah Isle of Wight yachting type — joined the Black Watch as a private. During his basic training, he was unwise enough to ask his drill sergeant, in his nonchalant Cowes Week drawl, whether all this jumping into mud and swinging on ropes was really necessary.

The sergeant stared at him for a long moment, then came close and hissed into his ear:

'I can stand cunts. I can even stand ignorant cunts. But I hates *educated* ones.'

An American magazine editor recently received a phone call from that self-important novelist Mordecai Richler.

'Hi Dick . . . Mordecai here.'

'Mordecai who?' the editor inquired.

President Calvin Coolidge was notoriously dry and taciturn. At a banquet in Washington, a young woman seated next to him determined to captivate him.

'Mr President,' she said brightly, 'I've made a bet with a friend that I can get you to say three words this evening.'

'You lose,' replied the President.

In later years, Mrs Patrick Campbell used to look at herself in the mirror and softly lament, 'O *why* must I look like a squashed paper bag?'

After the accidental drowning of a chronically obnoxious Thirties male movie idol off Malibu, Dorothy Parker was heard to wonder how one might send a telegram of congratulation to the Pacific Ocean.

In Liverpool, those not over-endowed with physical beauty are sometimes said to have 'a face like a ruptured custard.'

Disraeli was once forced to sit through an especially dismal banquet when every one of the numerous courses arrived at the table cold.

As the champagne was served he was heard to murmur, 'Thank Heaven for something warm at last.'

When, at the height of the Watergate scandal, several lawyers and aides joined Richard Nixon's embattled White House, a Washington observer remarked it was the first example on record of rats joining a sinking ship.

A friend lately disappointed in love was described to me by his somewhat unsympathetic younger brother as 'going round looking like a depressed hedgehog in search of a lorry.'

Notice in Sunday colour magazine concourse:
  'The Editor's indecision is final.'

The New York Post *headlined its review of a poor new play by Clifford Odets:*
             ODETS WHERE IS THY STING?

An Irish malediction goes:
  'If you was in Hell, Dante wouldn't piss on you.'

At studio boss Harry Cohn's funeral, his old enemy Jerry Wald was noticed among the congregation.

'Nice of you to come and pay your respects to Harry,' another mourner commented to Wald.

'Respects nothin',' Wald snapped. 'I just came to make sure the bastard's really dead.'

G. B. Shaw did not care much for conventional society. On one occasion he received a handsomely engraved card, vouchsafing that the Hon. Mrs So-and-so, on such-and-such a date, would be 'At home'.

Shaw returned the card with the handwritten message 'So will GBS.'

Alexander Walker on a dire Sixties movie version of *Alfred the Great*:

'It's a pity they left out the burning of the cakes. It's even more of a pity they left out the burning of the script.'

Hugh M. Hefner, during his years of pyjama-clad party-giving, used to be secretly referred to by *Playboy* magazine executives as 'Godzilla of Sleepy Hollow.'

Shelley Berman used to describe a Boy Scout troop as 'a lot of boys dressed as jerks, led by a jerk dressed as a boy.'

After Edward VII died, his body was left overnight at Buckingham Palace before being removed for lying-in-state. His widow, Queen Alexandra, kept vigil with a lady-in-waiting.

At one point Queen Alexandra remarked to the lady-in-waiting that it was the first night for many years when she'd known exactly where he was.

The gilded nymph adorning the ornamental clock of Northern Goldsmiths Ltd in Newcastle-upon-Tyne is known locally as 'Cunt on tick.'

Valediction of disenchanted New York lover:
*   'Don't move . . . I want to forget you just the way you are at this moment.'*

In Dr Johnson's time, the Thames boatmen were notorious for the insults they shouted at their passengers.

One man, unwise enough to shout at the Doctor, was answered with full Johnsonian majesty:

'Sir, your wife, under pretence of keeping a bawdy house, is a receiver of stolen goods.'

The most damningly succinct theatre review ever is commonly agreed to have been Walter Kerr's, after the Broadway opening of *I Am A Camera*:

'Me no Leica.'

In the Twenties, the *London Daily Graphic* came close with a two word notice of a new musical comedy called *Oh Yes!*:

'Oh No!'

The prize, however, goes to the *New Musical Express* in the mid-Seventies, reviewing the Abba album *Voulez Vous*.

The review consisted of one word:

'Non.'

Michael Foot once described Norman Tebbit as 'a semi-house-trained polecat.'

Ruby Wax on Joan Collins:
   'If it didn't have teeth to hold it up, that face would be wall-to-wall pucker.'

Janet Street-Porter recently described a noted London fashion journalist as 'looking like a cold chicken after someone's eaten all the best bits.'

'Ah Mr Shaw!' an Edwardian society beauty once exclaimed to GBS. 'We ought to get together and mate. Just think of producing a child with my looks and your brains!'
   'Oh, but dear lady . . .' Shaw demurred. 'Think of the disaster if it should turn out the other way round.'

A Southern candidate in the '76 Presidential election rather damaged his chances by remarking to a reporter that all coloured people wanted out of life was 'a tight fanny, loose shoes and a warm place to shit.'

While on the editing staff of the *New Yorker*, Alexander Woolcott was asked his opinion on a ponderous article entitled 'American Humor'.

'It seems to me', Woolcott wrote on the manuscript, 'this author has got American Humor down and broken its arm.'

Waiter to elderly clubman: 'Coffee, Sir?'

Elderly clubman: 'Ah . . . yes. I like my coffee like I like my women — hot, strong and sweet.'

Waiter: 'Yes, sir. Black or white?'

Christopher Booker wrote of a characteristic Alan Coren essay that it was 'a piece of homogenised facetiousness containing no observation whatever.'

A favourite schoolboy jibe:

Q: What's the difference between [name of unpopular teacher] and a bucket of shit?

A: The bucket.

Valediction of disenchanted New York lover:

'Always remember, if ever you're in trouble or lonely and need a friend . . . buy a dog.'

Cyril Connolly was once asked why, for all his acerbity as a critic, he was unfailingly generous about the literary productions of people he knew.

He replied, 'I would rather praise my friends' books than read them.'

Anthony Eden was said by a political opponent to have organised the 1956 Suez invasion 'to prove his moustache was real.'

A critic once wrote of Wilfrid Hyde-White that he'd spent the previous night's West End performance 'prowling round the stage looking for laughs with the single-mindedness of a tortoise on a lettuce-hunt.'

Nancy Banks-Smith once wrote of a certain TV actor that he had spent the previous night's performance standing around like a standard-lamp, and she had spent it longing to switch him off.

A caustic foreign editor was checking through the passport details of one of his less comely correspondents.

'"Distinguishing marks"' he read out. '"Scar tissue above right eyebrow". What about all the scar tissue *below* the right eyebrow?'

During the first era of surgical transplant miracles it was rumoured that Harold Wilson had had a bottom transplant — but that it had rejected him.

The newest torrid blockbuster by Sally Quin, wife of *Washington Post* editor Ben Bradlee, was famously summed up by *Vanity Fair*'s book critic as 'clitorature'.

The mother of my Liverpudlian friend Brenda Jones once referred to a family acquaintance as 'twopenn'orth of God-help-us wrapped up in a wet Echo.'

After Labour came to power in 1945, a disdainful Tory MP reported that he'd seen an empty taxi draw up outside the Commons and Mr Attlee get out.

Gault-Millau's New York restaurant inspector reports on having visited Tavern-on-the-Green and eaten a portion of banana cheesecake 'that would have smothered Desdemona quicker than her pillow.'

An elderly London clubman recently complained to the club secretary that the recent redecoration had made the place look like a Mayfair bordello.

'I must bow to your superior knowledge, Sir,' the secretary murmured.

Malcolm Muggeridge wrote of Anthony Eden that 'he did not merely bore — he bored for England.'

A few years ago, a film was made about the life of the Mitford sisters. Among the Mitfords themselves, the production was always referred to as '*La Triviata*'.

At the height of Orson Welles's fame in Hollywood, a gloomy studio publicist remarked, 'There but for the grace of God goes God.'

The husband of a Hollywood film goddess once saw his spouse looking glum.

'What's the matter, baby?' he inquired innocently.

'Nothing that getting divorced from you couldn't cure,' she replied.

On one occasion Noel Coward broke the golden rule that one should never write to a hostile critic.

'Dear —' his note began. 'Your review is before me. It will shortly be behind me.'

Sir Thomas Beecham's chastenings of inferior musicianship were known and relished throughout the orchestral world.

Once, he stopped a symphony orchestra in mid-rehearsal and gazed down at a female cellist whose playing had been unremittingly mediocre.

'Madam,' he said. 'Between your legs, God has put a treasure . . . and all you can do is sit there and scratch it.'

Sir Gerald Du Maurier was once buttonholed by an anxious would-be member of his club, the Garrick, hoping for news from the membership committee.

'Were there any blackballs in the voting?' the would-be member asked.

Sir Gerald drew him aside and murmured, 'My dear fellow . . . have you ever seen sheepshit?'

'Don't you think Frank Pakenham is the baldest man you've ever seen? Passionately *bald, in fact.'*

— *Malcolm Muggeridge*

Bob Hope used to say of a certain fellow actor that he'd been in so many B pictures, he was getting fanmail from hornets.

John Zametica wrote of Herbert Morrison that the private papers he'd left behind were so dull and banal, 'they might as well be burned if they are to provide any illumination at all.'

John Kenneth Galbraith was recently described in The Spectator *as 'the most famous living Canadian after Margaret Trudeau.'*

The late Diana Dors had a quick way with lechers and fumblers. At a party a few years ago, a man lurched up to her and mumbled, 'Coo . . . . I'd really like to *fuck* you.'

Ms Dors turned to him, took in his modest stature, then frowned and wagged a reproving forefinger.

'If you do,' she said, 'and I find out about it . . .'

The misanthropic W. C. Fields once received an invitation to play golf with a Hollywood producer he disliked.

'No thanks,' he replied. 'If I ever want to play with a prick, I'll play with my own.'

A nineteenth century critic wrote of William Morris that he was 'a great all-round talent — the trouble is, it takes much too long to walk all round him.'

Stanley Baldwin was said by a Parliamentary opponent to have 'all the power and presence of a hole in the air.'

The staff of a certain highly impressionable and mercurial Fleet Street editor used to say that his face always bore the impression of the latest bottom to have sat on it.

A New York woman is proudly telling friends how she has just managed to shed 250 pounds of unsightly fat: she got divorced.

A political commentator summed up Harold Wilson's chief Prime Ministerial quality, in three administrations, as 'an undeviating lack of candour.'

I was once told by a Liverpudlian that I was 'as useless as a one-legged man in an arse-kicking contest.'

Pop gossip item on Capital radio:
'Alison Moyet's heading for the sun . . . Stand by for a total eclipse.'

The late Sir Ralph Richardson was described by a pre-war reviewer as 'the glass eye in the forehead of English acting.'

Malcolm Muggeridge has admitted in print that his initial estimation of David Frost was wrong:
'I thought he would sink without trace. But instead he rose without trace.'

Truman Capote's description of Dorothy Parker, from *Answered Prayers*:
'She was like a vulnerable child who'd gone to sleep and awakened forty years later with puffy eyes, false teeth and whisky on her breath.'

After Edward Heath published his book Sailing *in 1975, The Times diarist suggested the title of its sequel might, perhaps, be 'Failing'.*

On a recent Joan Rivers TV show, Bernard Manning told Rupert Everett, 'If brains were dynamite, you'd not have enough to blow your hat off.'

He went on to remark that Everett was 'about as much fun as woodworm in a cripple's crutch.'

～

A theatre critic once described Glenda Jackson as 'the face that launched a thousand dredgers.'

～

Sybil Colefax irritated many in Thirties society by knowing everything about everybody. Or, as Margot Asquith put it, 'One cannot talk about the birth of Christ without that astrakhan idiot saying she was there in the manger.'

～

The New York magazine Gentleman's Quarterly is known for short as GQ but more commonly — in tribute to its main readership — as Geriatric Queens.

～

When *Penthouse* magazine first began to challenge the huge worldwide sales of *Playboy*, a columnist in *Time* remarked that on Hugh Hefner's hitherto clear horizon there had appeared 'a cloud no larger than a man's hand.'

～

Victoria Wood recently wrote that her nose has lately grown so big, the rest of her face is applying for a Council flat.

After his series of Royal interviews for 'News at Ten',
Sir Alistair Burnet is said to be the only man in England
whose trousers wear out at the knee.

Sunday Times *critic John Peter described* The Phantom
of the Opera *as 'Masked Balls'.*

Zsa Zsa Gabor said that one of her latter marriages had
been 'a love-hate relationship.'
   'He loved me, I hated him.'

The Guardian *once headlined a review of a notably*
rotten production of Antony and Cleopatra:
   THE BIGGEST ASP DISASTER IN THE WORLD

'I love this club. It's like home to me — filthy and full
of strangers.'

— Ronnie Scott on Ronnie Scott's

Arthur Scargill is reputedly one of the few people who
can manage three Shredded Wheats at breakfast.
   He eats two and puts the third one on his head.

It's said at Oxford and Cambridge that one can always
spot an undergraduate rower by the scar on the head
where the brain's been removed.

The film critic Michael Pye recently described Sylvester Stallone as 'twelve million bucks worth of cows' eyes and mumbling.'

Sitting through Stallone's latest film *Cobra*, went on Pye, had been 'like being run over by a convoy of manure trucks.'

Alister Ross

... accompanied here – by virtue of a surrealist experiment in the bookbinder's craft – by YOUR WALRUS HURT THE ONE YOU LOVE, an assembly of malapropisms, mispronunciations and linguistic cock-ups with contributions from the Princess of Wales, President Reagan, John Lennon, Thor Heyerdahl and a legion of linguistically inept British cleaning ladies. Philip Norman has discovered the middle-aged man undergoing "a mid-wife crisis" and friends who go to Israel to live on a "kebab", a devout Catholic convinced that the Pope is "inflammable" and aircraft emitting "masonic" bangs, the doctor asked if he could hear anything through his "horoscope" and the London pub serving "boiled god in parsley sauce". Here is the quintessential art of the wrong word in the wrong place as practised by elderly aunts, small children, and TV sports commentators.

A modest exercise in manual dexterity will reveal that YOUR WALRUS HURT THE ONE YOU LOVE is ...

BY THE SAME AUTHOR

Novels

Slip On A Fat Lady
`Plumridge
The Skaters' Waltz
Wild Thing (short stories)

Biography and Journalism

Shout: The True Story of the Beatles
The Stones
The Road Goes On For Ever
Tilt the Hourglass and Begin Again

Plays

The Man That Got Away
Skiffle

Your Walrus Hurt
The One You Love

Malapropisms, mispronunciations
and linguistic cock-ups.

Philip Norman

PAPERMAC

This collection copyright © 1988 by Philip Norman

Your Walrus Hurt the One You Love copyright © 1985 by Philip Norman

illustrations copyright © 1985 by Marie-Hélène Jeeves
Awful Moments copyright © 1986 by Philip Norman
illustrations copyright © 1986 by Marie-Hélène Jeeves
Pieces of Hate copyright © 1987 by Philip Norman
illustrations copyright © 1987 by Paula Youens

All rights reserved. No reproduction, copy or transmission of this publication may be made without written permission. No paragraph of this publication may be reproduced, copied or transmitted save with written permission or in accordance with the provisions of the Copyright Act 1956 (as amended). Any person who does any unauthorised act in relation to this publication may be liable to criminal prosecution and civil claims for damages.

This collection first published 1988 by
PAPERMAC
a division of Macmillan Publishers Limited
4 Little Essex Street London WC2R 3LF
and Basingstoke

Associated companies in Auckland, Delhi, Dublin, Gaborone, Hamburg, Harare, Hong Kong, Johannesburg, Kuala Lumpur, Lagos, Manzini, Melbourne, Mexico City, Nairobi, New York, Singapore and Tokyo

British Library Cataloguing in Publication Data
Norman, Philip
The Norman trilogy
I. Title II. Norman, Philip. Your walrus hurt the one you love.
Norman Philip. Awful moments. Norman, Philip. Pieces of hate.
828'.91402'08

ISBN: 0-333-47447-X

Printed in Hong Kong

Your Walrus Hurt the One You Love, Awful Moments and *Pieces of Hate* were first published as separate volumes by Elm Tree Books, London, in 1985, 1986 and 1987 respectively.
Cover design by Marie-Hélène Jeeves

Contents

Introduction

When Sheridan's Mrs Malaprop irritably complained that Lydia Languish was as 'headstrong as an allegory on the banks of the Nile', she was not inventing, merely mal-appropriating the foible that bears her name. Two centuries earlier in *Much Ado About Nothing*, Dogberry the constable had proudly 'comprehended two aspicious persons' at the head of his 'dissembly'. Other figures in literature are at least the stately dame's equal at speaking *mal apropos*. In Smollett's *Humphry Clinker*, Mrs Winifred Jenkins threatens to succumb to a fit of 'asterisks'. Mincing, the maid in Congreve's *Way of the World*, announces that dinner is 'impatient'. We would speak of Dogberries, Jenkinses, Mincings (or, for that matter, Bottoms, Mistress Quicklies, even Pecksniffs or Gamps) if there were any justice in literature. But let it pass: as Dogberry observes elsewhere, 'comparisons are odorous'.

The fact is that the English are a nation of malapropists and that our language in its richest parts derives from our reluctance to pronounce any word — especially any foreign

1

word — correctly, if we can help it. The urge to malaprop arises from three fine old English qualities. The first is unrepentant ignorance. The second is contempt for other races. The third is the steadfast belief that whatever any English person says must be right. Add to

this our love of pun and conundrum and our deeply-ingrained embarrassment about organised religion, and you can see how 'bloody' as an oath mutated from the sacrilegious 'By Our Lady', or how a tavern named after the Infanta of Castile ended up as the Elephant and Castle.

This book owes its origin to a slow week on the *Sunday Times* Atticus column, when I casually invited readers to send in their favourite malapropism. The result kept the column going — and its editor semi-hysterical — for three consecutive weeks. The letters, ratting on grandmothers, aunts, parents, children, employers, spouses and lovers, were uniformly affectionate. Malapropists, I realise, are beloved members of society, cherished by the people they so unwittingly entertain. Part of the sublime innocence that launches them into their mid-air verbal collisions and linguistic pratfalls is never realising how many aficionados are standing by, hanging on to their every pulverised word.

Since leaving Atticus, I have gone on collecting examples from friends, colleagues and correspondents all over Britain and America. In making this selection, I have discarded mere hapless puns and concentrated on the flights of brilliant alternative imagery that distinguish the truly inspired malapropist. I happen to have the sort of mind that would rather believe that curtains hang from a 'pelvis', that men in evening dress hold their trousers up with a 'camembert' and that

children in World War II were saved from the London blitz by being 'evaporated'. Not that these verbal Dalis deal only in the fantastical. Greater truth than they know may be spoken by malapropists who come to you with the 'mucus' of an idea, or describe how they 'hee'd and hawed' before buying something because the price was so 'exuberant'. An incidental joy has been to discover how little the glorious urge is a respecter of class or profession. I was recently shown a letter to a New York publisher from a high-powered literary agent, confidently vouchsafing that his client's new novel was 'jettisoned' for the best-seller list.

Where malapropisms blur into spoonerism, mixed metaphor or double entendre, I have allowed them to blur. What's the good of doing something like this if one can't be a *little* self-divulgent?

Philip Norman, New York, 1985

4

Grateful thanks to Peter Miln, Ned Sherrin, Tracey Norman, Ronald Mansbridge, George Brock, John Young and readers of *The Times* and *The New York Times Book Review*.

'Just a lot of belladonnas . . .'

Malapropisms of the Mighty

President Ronald Reagan's reliance on cue-cards which his contact lenses sometimes cannot fully distinguish makes him a malapropist *par excellence*. The other month he demonstrated the fact yet again at a White House reception by introducing President Samuel Doe of Liberia to the American nation as 'Chairman Moe'. In another famous speech, grasping for a Biblical allusion to support nuclear proliferation, the President attempted to say 'Samson slew the Philistines' but actually said 'Simpson slew the Philippines'.

The late Lord Drogheda, when chairman of the *Financial Times*, coined a fine double-header in describing the mix-up over two paintings in a friend's ancestral home. What had been thought to be a Tintoretto proved on examination to be a Canaletto. 'They thought it was a Rio Tinto,' his Lordship explained. 'Now they've discovered it's a Rigoletto.'

During the visit of President John F. Kennedy and his fashionable young wife to Paris in 1962, a new word became the vogue among the White House press corps — 'treasurely'. Everything in Paris, the correspondents told one another, was 'just too treasurely'.

The word is said to have derived from Jackie Kennedy's remark on visiting the Louvre and seeing the Mona Lisa:

'Oh — it's très jolie.'

John Lennon was as much a malapropist by accident as a punster by design. George Martin, the Beatles' record producer, remembers taking Lennon to dinner in a restaurant when he was first down from Liverpool. A waiter approached with a dish and murmured 'Mange-tout, Sir?' 'Okay,' Lennon agreed cautiously, 'but put 'em over there, not anywhere near the food.'

An earnest BBC interviewer once asked Lennon if in his writing he made 'conscious use of onomatopoeia'.

'I dunno what that feller was on about,' Lennon said later. 'He kept on talking about an automatic pier.'

Lord Blyton, the 84-year-old former MP for Durham, was asked by a journalist how he rated his fellow peers' performance in the first televised Lords debate.

'Waste of time,' he muttered. 'They're all just a lot of belladonnas.'

America's most renowned civic malapropist was the terrible Mayor Richard Daley of Chicago. In 1968, after Daley's police had run amok through the Democratic party convention, the Mayor appeared on television to refute charges of unnecessary violence. 'I'll say just one thing on this,' Daley began in his accustomed Irish bellow. 'It's the police's job to preserve disorder. And they *preserved* disorder . . .'

On a lighter occasion, the Mayor was invited to endorse the riding of tandems as a way of promoting harmony between married couples. Daley performed an unsteady circuit on the rear of a tandem, then came to the waiting microphones.

'I just wanna say,' he bellowed, 'you husbands and wives, if you wanna get along together, you gotta get one of these tantrum bicycles . . .'

An NUM official, interviewed on Radio 4 after the year-long miners' strike, angrily described the National Coal Board as 'totally incontinent'.

The Princess of Wales, opening a new hospital wing in Northamptonshire — at a time when National Health malingering was much in the news — said she hoped the new facility would be used by people 'lying in the district'.

An NUM official described the National Coal
Board as totally incontinent . . .

While running for President in 1971, Alabama's white supremist Governor George Wallace realised he must strike a chord of brotherhood with the Negro voter.

'Sure, ah look like a white man . . .' Wallace told a large assembly of his prospective brothers. 'But mah heart is as black as anybody's heah.'

The utterances of Samuel Goldwyn showed to what height the malapropism could be taken by huge Philistinism married to enormous power. 'A verbal agreement's not worth the paper it's written on' summed up the great film mogul's business ethos. A suggestion that he should show charity to a competitor, who happened to be an old friend, was dismissed by the pragmatic reflection, 'We've passed a lot of water under the bridge since then.'

At critical moments, Goldwyn was apt to warn his subordinates that MGM studios stood 'on the brink of an abscess'. Informed there was a dearth of Indian extras in a new Western epic, he brusquely ordered, 'Get some more from the reservoir.'

On a rare occasion, a new production his subordinates had praised as 'magnificent' stirred Samuel Goldwyn to the depths. 'It's more than magnificent,' he said. 'It's *mediocre*!'

In 1980, the word-strangling General Alexander Haig declined to answer a Senate Committee question on the grounds that it was 'too suppository'.

A Baloney Amputation

Nothing inspires people to malapropism with quite the same intensity as the subject of their own health. It appears an essential human impulse, not merely to mishear one's doctor's diagnosis but to accept it as gospel, however bizarre it may sound, and be positively proud of the challenge it poses to medical science.

'My doctor says I've got acute vagina.'

'It's the old man's disease — my prophylactic gland.'

'They're sending me in next week for my hysterical rectum.'

'I've got to have my aviaries removed.'

'I've had stomach pains for months. The specialist says it could be an ulster.'

James Lees-Milne's diaries record how the American-born London socialite Laura Corrigan astounded her salon with what she presumed a routine piece of medical advice.

'My doctor told me, "If you want to avoid indigestion, you must masturbate, masturbate. . . ."'

'If you want to avoid indigestion . . .'

My Cockney grandmother, back from a visit to her sister in hospital, feelingly described the 'sirloin' drip attached to the patient's arm. It had been difficult to talk, my grandmother said, with all the doctors 'hoovering' around. Nonetheless, she was reassured that her sister seemed to be receiving 'the RIP treatment'.

 Barbara Sachs of Rickmansworth recalls that her GP husband was frequently asked by his Cockney patients for a 'stiff ticket' to get off work.

14

One patient he was examining inquired, 'Tell me, doc — can you really hear anything through that horoscope?'

Dr Michael Reilly, of Yelverton, Devon, tells me of the surrealistic surgical enterprises that can result when hospital typists give approximate phonetic renderings of the medical terms dictated to them.

Dr Reilly remembers a report on a Barium meal X-ray for stomach ulcers which stated — suitably enough in the West Country — that the patient's interior revealed 'a phantom pasty', rather than the faint opacity the specialist had noticed.

On another occasion, Dr Reilly found

himself listed to perform a 'baloney amputation' instead of the below-knee one he had anticipated.

While serving as a corporal in the Royal Army Medical Corps, J. Forrest Penman, of Edinburgh, looked searchingly at a soldier on sick parade and asked what he was complaining of.

'I've got a swelling in my grotto, Corp,' the man replied.

A Washington paediatrician reports that children in her care consciously use malapropisms to make the medical terms they overhear seem less intimidating. The unpleasant bone marrow test for leukaemia has thus become converted into 'the bow and arrow test'. Spinal meningitis is known by the far more companionable name 'Smiling Mighty Jesus'.

A frequent feminine anxiety confided to Dr Alex Sakula, of Reigate, is: 'Doctor, I'm afraid I must be suffering from the mental pause.'

Dr John Trowell, of Sawbridgeworth, Herts, remembers treating a patient who brought with him a diagnosis from the 'Reptile Clinic' (Rectal Clinic).

The diagnosis was 'fissure in ano' — or, as the patient himself rendered it, 'fish in ano'.

A telephone caller to a Gloucestershire hospital baffled the switchboard operator by

asking for 'Sir Michael Spears'. It transpired that what she wanted was 'Cervical Smears'.

Jean Prickett of Tenterden, Kent, remembers this sad confidence from a male acquaintance:

'Unfortunately, we can never have children. My wife is inconceivable.'*

In the days of government-issue National Dried milk, a midwife advised that a baby, doing badly with its mother's milk, should be 'put on the Grand National'. Another such prescient soul urged that, to avoid risk of diphtheria, the baby should forthwith be 'humanised'.

A London hospital orderly was sent to the stores for a spiggot to be fitted at the end of a patient's catheter. The storekeeper could make nothing of his statement that Mrs so-and-so's tube needed 'a spinnaker'.

My Washington informant remembers treating a black woman patient who was complaining of menstrual discomfort.

'How's your flow?' the doctor asked.

'Pretty good since I started with that new wax polish,' the patient replied.

C. C. Lindsay of Croydon remembers an old family retainer who went to the doctor

*The male malapropist cause of this problem is 'being impudent'.

17

complaining of stomach pains, and was much cheered by the diagnosis. 'I've got a slight structure,' she said. 'But it's all right — I shan't have to wear a trestle.'

A Royal Navy doctor's mother proudly tells her friends that her son has now attained the rank of 'Surging Lieutenant Commander'.

The semi-retired senior partner in a Walton-on-Thames medical practice recently heard himself described by one of his patients as 'semi-retarded'.

Worried that a swimmer might get into difficulties off the beach near her house, Brenda Dorley-Brown of Seaview, Isle of Wight, asked her local doctor for some basic instruction in administering 'the Kiss of Death'.

A colleague of Peter Hayes, Gloucestershire County Council's Information Officer, told him she could never use talcum powder because it pored her clogs.

News reaches me of these further alarming medical mishaps and predicaments:

Of a swimmer revived from drowning by 'artificial insemination'.

Of a birth by the painful 'Cistercian' method.

Of a man over 40 experiencing 'a midwife crisis'.

Of a vasectomy patient who wondered if he would ever have 'martial' relations again.

Of the New York woman admitted to an eye hospital for an operation on her 'Cadillacs'.

Of the Florida lady, fearful of childbirth, who, while making love with her husband, obliged him to wear a 'condominium'.

Of a family friend whose doctor tells her she is 'a little obeast'.

Of patients suffering variously from 'teutonic' ulcers, 'malingering' tumours and 'congenial' heart disease.

Of the sane person mistakenly admitted to a 'menthol' hospital.

Of the accident victim who, having severed 'the juggler vein' . . . 'bled like a stuffed pig'.

Of the back sufferer who had lost faith in manipulation by her 'octopus', and — though she feared the needles might hurt — was determined to discover if any relief could be obtained by 'acapulco'.

I hear of horticultural malapropists who proudly exhibit their 'spitoonias', 'enemas' and dahlia 'tumours', and whose great fear, as they nurture their potato crop, is the return of that dread 1950s pest, the 'Corduroy' beetle.

Michael Reilly remembers an old gardener in Plymouth during the World War 2 bombing, who was outraged at the damage done to grassland by 'insanitary' [incendiary] bombs.

Mrs D. Tomlin, of Aylesbury, complimented an elderly gardening neighbour on the wonderful show he had produced. 'Ah —' he said, 'and you know, it's the first time I ever tried growing these here Christian anthems.'

Peter Miln tells me of a postman in Staffordshire, who was much struck by the clematis entwined around the front porch of a house on his route.

'It looks really pretty,' he said to the householder, 'now your wife's got her clitoris to climb all up round there.'

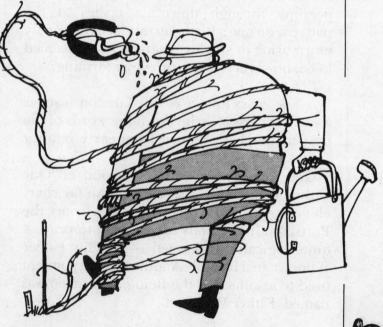

'It looks really pretty now your wife's got her clitoris to climb all up round there . . .'

'Christ the Royal Master leans against the phone . . .'

Childhood's malapropisms stay with one for ever, none more so than those arising from hymns, prayers and the general notion of Heaven, Jesus and God. Who does not remember standing in school assembly, peeping through downcast lashes at the patterns on one's Birthday sandals, resignedly murmuring or singing what the words seemed to be, however strange or even alarming?

A few years ago, a North London teacher asked his class to write down the words of the prayer they had intoned from early infancy at least once a day.

One small boy's written version of 'Our Father Who art in Heaven' was 'Ah far chart eleven. . .' A correspondent from the Portsmouth area tells me he used to pray — quite logically, it seemed — to 'Our Father Who art in Havant'. Another correspondent used to assume that the Being in Heaven was named 'Father Whichart'.

The next line has been interpreted by children since Victorian times as 'Harold be

'Hello, breathe Thy name'

Thy name' — or, in the murmurous slur of voices, a cordial but cautious greeting, 'Hello . . . breathe Thy name.' Julia Denison-Smith, from BFPO 15, tells me her small son's version of the line after that was 'Give us this day our day in bed.'

'Lead us not into temptation' assumes new significance among children from London riverside boroughs as 'Lead us not into Thames Station'. J. R. Chester of South Croydon remembers that, when he employed a rather disagreeable German au pair girl, his small son would go on to say, 'But deliver us from Eva.'

23

Philip Brough of Aberdare tells me he used to assume, when his upper class infants teacher said, 'Thine is the Kingdom, the Pa and the Glory', that 'The Pa' was yet another confusing reference to Our Father.

Psalm 23 has always been noted for its striking imagery. 'The Lord is my Shepherd, I shall not want. He maketh me to lie down in green parsley . . . He leadeth me beside distilled waters . . .' And the final, rather worrying reflection: 'Surely Good Mrs Murphy shall follow me all the days of my life . . .'

Hymns have produced such exotic personages as 'Round John Virgin' (featured with mother and child in 'Silent Night'), and the time-honoured 'Gladly, my cross-eyed bear'.

To Mrs M. M. Rotheram, of Guildford, it used to seem no more than prudent that the concluding entreaty of 'Away in a Manger' was 'Stay by my cider till morning is nigh.' A little girl in Elaine Bishop's Totnes Sunday School class used to ask for 'the hymn about the nighties' — 'Now the day is over, nighties drawing near.' Ernest Pratt of West Kirby, Wirral, remembers his four-year-old son's lusty paean to 'All things bright and beautiful, our teachers great and small'. Not to be outdone was Michael Reilly's small niece, in

the chorus of 'Onward Christian Soldiers', when she sang 'Christ the Royal Master leans against the phone.'

The Rev. J. H. Davies of Southampton was told by his mother that she used to think the *Gloria Patri* was about a naughty little girl named Glory — hence 'Glory beat the Father, ran to the Son, ran to the Holy Ghost.' Suzanne Beven of Esher remembers always being rather frightened by references to 'The Father, The Son and the Holy Ghosty men'. There is also the story of the small boy, holding a burial service for a dead bird, who cheerily intoned: 'In the name of the Father and of the Son . . . and into the 'ole he goes . . .'

Eric Taylor of Reigate knows a small girl who firmly believed the opening words of Handel's *Messiah* were: 'Come for tea, come for tea my people saith your God . . .'

A Sunday School teacher in Sussex discovered that, when her class repeated The Creed, most believed that Jesus had suffered, not under Pontius Pilate but under 'a bunch of spiders'.

A little boy from Basingstoke, Hampshire, came home from Sunday School and told his

parents he had been learning about St Paul's conversion on the Domestos Road.

A little girl from Abbots Bromley, Staffordshire, told her mother in great excitement that the prizes at her school speech day were to be presented by 'The Archdemon of Stoke'.

A little boy in Worcestershire thought, with unimpeachable logic, that the Seventh Commandment was 'Thou shalt not come into Dudley.'

As a boy chorister at his local church, R. D. Widdas of South Croydon used to be mystified by the frequent appeals for contributions to 'the Vicar's Tiepin Fund'.

So his youthful ears interpreted 'the Vicar's Stipend Fund'.

The voice of Nat 'King' Cole singing 'Unforgettable' comes back to me from the age of ten or so. The singer's distinctive phrasing seemed to me at one point to spoil the song's mood of unalloyed admiration. I thought he was singing, not 'That's why darling, it's incredible . . .' but *'That's* my darling. It's incredible!' Likewise on Billy Eckstine's 'I Apologise' — bearing in mind my mother's betting proclivities — I thought the line 'If I told a lie . . .' was 'If I totalised . . .'

Modern popular songs, if anything, give greater scope for childish misunderstanding. I hear of a small girl fan of the Three Degrees who skipped round her house singing the refrain 'Bicycle hut' rather than 'My simple heart'; and of another who firmly believed 'Way Down Yonder in New Orleans' to be a song about 'three old ladies with flashing eyes', the notion of Creole ladies being too exotic for her to grasp.

In the Sixties Beat Boom, it was widely believed among children that the chorus to Gerry and the Pacemakers' biggest hit ran: 'You give me a feeling in my heart/like a marrow passing through it'. And that Clarence

'Frogman' Henry's big ballad hit of 1961 was not 'You Always Hurt The One You Love' but 'Your Walrus Hurt The One You Love'.

'I do like it when you smile,' an affectionate little girl told her mother. 'It shows the plimsolls in your cheeks.'

. . . the plimsolls in your cheeks . . .

A little boy in Hull was proud of the fact that whenever Kojak, the TV detective, picked up the phone in his office, he invariably seemed to be saying 'Hello . . . Humberside.'

Kojak was, of course, saying in his brusque New York way, 'Hello . . . Homicide . . .'

A little girl in Newcastle-on-Tyne firmly

believed that Elizabeth Taylor lived in Gateshead, rather than Gstaad.

A little girl recently arrived in New York to live told a friend how long she and her mother had had to wait in a department store before the 'alligator' arrived to take them to the fifth floor.

A little boy in Minneapolis was asked by his mother why his friend Brandon never came over to play at his house.

'Brandon can't come here,' the boy replied. 'He's a homosexual.'

On closer examination, he explained he thought a homosexual was someone who only liked being at home.

A little girl in Northamptonshire wrote home from her first boarding school to say that the headmistress had 'calved' at Sunday lunch.

A little boy in Devon said he had not liked to see his mother at the beauty parlour with 'crawlers' in her hair.

A little girl in North London told her teacher that someone had just been to her house to fit the doors and windows with 'giraffe-excluders'.

A little girl of eight had just received a severe scolding from her father, but was determined not to give way to tears. 'That's *it*, Daddy,' she said, scarlet-faced. 'Now I've really taken Uxbridge!'

From school and student essay and examination papers:

'*The three ways of transmitting heat are conduction, conviction and constipation.*'

'*King Henry disguised himself in the garbage of a monk . . .*'

'*This poem begins in medeas rex . . .*'

'*Samson felled a thousand foreskins.*'

Conduction, conviction and constipation . . .

'*St Paul was persecuted by the Emperor Nehru.*'

'*A musket was a most unweedy weapon . . .*'

'*The practice of having only one wife is called monotony.*'

'*Socrates died from an overdose of wedlock.*'

'*Isaac Newton was very studious as a child, when he could often be found embossed in a book.*'

'*A virgin forest is a place where the hand of man has never set foot.*'

'*Eugene O'Neill's greatest achievement was winning the Pullet Surprise.*'*

*Pulitzer Prize

Winning the Pullet Surprise

'Russia uses the acrylic alphabet.'

'At Lord Nelson's funeral, it took 50 sailors to carry the beer.'

'King George lay in state for two days on a catapult.'

'Pompeii was destroyed by an overflow of red hot saliva.'

'The Equator is a menagerie lion running round the Earth.'

'After the baby butterfly has been a caterpillar, it becomes a syphilis.'

'Salome did the Dance of the Seven Veils in front of Harrods.'

Ned Sherrin tells me of a young actress named Chrissie Kendall who is undisputedly the Mrs Malaprop of the contemporary stage. In Sherrin's hearing recently, she spoke about a friend who had gone off to Israel to live on 'a kebab'. She also habitually refers to the Royal Shakespeare Company as 'the RAC'.

During 1979, her colleagues heard her express mounting concern over 'the ostriches'.

'What ostriches?' a friend inquired.

'The ostriches in prison in Iran,' Ms Kendall replied.

An Appetising Camisole

The lady who attributed her tasty meat dishes to a plentiful infusion of 'spies and bailiffs' — spices and bay leaves — made the point well enough. Good cooks have too much else on their plates to be bothered with words. And why should they? Would those 'spies' taste any the worse for being ground up, as the

same lady said, with a 'pedestal' and mortar? Would a stew not be rather the more appetising for having been simmered at length in an antique 'camisole'? Would one not really prefer to believe in traditional British dishes like 'knockers and mash' or newly popular continental ones like 'camel only'? Only vegetarians could object — and for them there is always the 'mackerel-biotic' diet.

Standbys from the malapropist's store cupboard

Fruit compost
Canine pepper
Desecrated coconut
Tomato catspit
Ogre beans*
Exasperated (or paralysed) milk

Wednesday daily cheese
Nipplepolitan ice cream
Smoky bunion crisps
Peanut bristle

*Aubergines. Not to be confused with primitive people in Australia.

35

'She is an excellent cook, clean and good-tempered. She is leaving us of her own violation.'
—*Employer's reference, 1930s*

Mary Carter, of Cambridge, remembers a cook who worked for her sister in Gloucestershire and who swore by the old Home & Colonial Stores. When she ran short of something, she would say, 'I'll have to pop out to the Holy Cologne.'

An elderly New York lady refused her granddaughter's cold leek and potato soup with a true Jewish cook's distaste both for its consistency and its outlandish French name.
'No thank you, dear,' she said. 'I don't care for that Vishy-vashy stuff.'

A 'county' mother in Cambridgeshire has been telling friends proudly that her daughter has been accepted for a course at the 'Condom Bleu'.

Sylvia Howard, a chef in Virginia Water, was recently conferring with the supervisor of the hotel cleaning crew.
'If there's any change in the schedule,' the supervisor said, 'I'll be sure to lyonnaise with you.'

The proprietor of a Staffordshire bistro remembers being asked by a customer if wine was served 'by the giraffe'.

The CO of a well-known British regiment is cherished by his junior officers for having once remarked that, what with his love of food and wine and the good things in life, he supposed he was 'a bit of a sodomite'.

A Sloane Ranger and her poorer friend, searching for a cheap place to eat, happened on the Bloomsbury trattoria Mille Pini.

'What about this?' the friend said jocularly. 'A thousand pines.'

'Oh, *no*,' the Sloane Ranger protested. 'It *can't* be as expensive as all that!'

Out on a heavy date, a rash young Londoner asked his companion if she would like to finish their Italian meal with that romantic liqueur which comes in glasses with blue fire licking around the rim.

Calling the waiter, he ordered 'two coffees and two Osso Bucos'.

A haggis-maker named Mr McSween recently confided to the *Meat Trades Journal* that he has 'a gut feeling' that he will soon open his own haggis factory.

The *Sunday Times Magazine* reported in the sixties that when cookery writer Margaret Costa bought a special cut of veal for 'a feast from Valhalla . . . she stuffed it personally with Mr Duckett of Harrods Meat Department.'

The mother of a London advertising man was about to set off for her first ever holiday in Cyprus. 'Whatever you do,' her son counselled, 'you mustn't miss trying the moussaka.'

His mother looked guarded.

'Well, if I don't have any while I'm there,' she said, 'I'll be sure to bring a bottle home.'

A Greek waiter in London extolled the night's special dishes thus: 'I have got stifado and I have got meaty balls.'

Some enticing dishes noted on menus throughout the world

'Stuffed nun'	(*Indian restaurant, Paddington, London*)
'Kidneys of the chef	(*Cathedral restaurant, Granada, Spain*)
'Smoked Solomon'	(*Intercontinental Hotel, Jakarta*)
'Turdy Delight'	(*seafront restaurant, Eilat, Israel*)
'Pig in the family way'	(*available throughout West Germany*)
'Terminal soup'	(*Istanbul airport cafeteria*)

'Steamed dick with vegetables'	*(Chinese restaurant, Gerrard St, London)*
'Quick Lorraine'	*(pub in Ebury St, London)*
'Roast Headlamp'*	*(taverna in Patmos, Greece)*
'Squits with source'	*(restaurant in Gassin, Alpes-Maritimes)*
'Boiled god in parsley'	*(pub in Covent Garden, London)*

*'Head of lamb'

'Calve's dong'	(*Hydra Taverna, Athens*)
'Fish Rotty and spaghetti Boldeveloped'	(*hotel in North Yemen*)
'Battered soul'	(*Ashoka Hotel, New Delhi*)
'Fried Brian'	(*Plat du jour, Geneva, Switzerland*)
'Hard-boiled eggs, filled with a delicate curried mouse'	(*Bistro blackboard, Manchester*)

A Stretcher Named Desire

Staff in the better bookshops tend to become adept at interpreting the bizarre titles for which they are asked by malapropist customers. They know, for instance, that 'Silent Mourner' is the common malaprop version of *Silas Marner*; that 'June the Obscure' will be stocked under H for Hardy; and that anyone seeking 'A Stretcher Named Desire' should be directed to the American drama section.

Valiantly sympathetic sales assistants, both sides of the Atlantic, have unscrambled 'Son of Siriasis' into *The Sun Also Rises*, deduced 'The Fruits of Anger' to mean *The Grapes of Wrath*, and eventually comprehended that 'Freddy The Rabbit Slept Late' was in fact the idiomatic Jewish novel *Friday the Rabbi Slept Late*.

A customer in a Chicago branch of B. Dalton recently caused total bafflement by asking if they stocked 'The Sauce'. Searches of the cookery section, and publishers' catalogues, could find nothing of that name.

What she wanted, it turned out, was Roget's Thesaurus.

Not long afterwards, another customer in the same store asked for Roget's Theodorakis.

41

Hatchards of Piccadilly tell me that the recent Hamish Hamilton biography *Horrocks: the General Who Led From the Front* was frequently asked for as 'Horrocks: the General Who Fled From the Front'.

A sedate publisher of hobby and handiwork books, some years ago, issued a series under the general title *Making It*. There was *Making It in Pottery; Making It in Fretwork; Making It in Glass* . . .

The publishers could not understand the huge extra sales that accrued to the volume called *Making It in Leather*.

Simon Bainbridge of Hatchards remembers being approached by a downtrodden-looking male customer, who showed him a piece of paper and said, 'My wife's asked me to get this. Do you stock it?'

On the paper was written 'Night Cream by Elizabeth Arden'.

'Remember — the Pope is inflammable . . .'

What survey of word-bungling can be complete without the Rev. Dr. Spooner and his 'piece of cod that passeth all understanding'? This original Spoonerism was, indeed, more malapropism, though Spooner went on to achieve technical perfection with his invocation of the 'Shoving Leopard'. Truth to tell, malapropism has been an essential in English worship since before Henry VIII dissolved the monasteries. Did you know that pubs called The Goat and Compasses were those which originally bore above their entrance the pious words 'God encompasseth us'?

Good News, the magazine of the Additional Curates Society, reports the complaint of an elderly worshipper who was finding it difficult to hear sermons even from the front pew:

'You'll have to come up to date and have microphones, Vicar. The agnostics in this church are very poor.'

The main speaker at a recent Anglican seminar on orthodox theology told his

audience of his belief that 'between Man and God there has been placed a vast abbess.'

A churchwarden's wife in the Midlands dramatically described what trouble had been caused in a local house by a poltergeist until the vicar was called in to 'circumcise' it.

A devout Catholic, in theological debate with some Anglican friends, produced the customary clinching argument:
'Ah, but what you must remember is that to us the Pope is inflammable.'

During the 1984 Coal Strike, a London vicar led his congregation in praying for 'reconciliation in the minefields'.

An old age pensioner in North London was continuing to struggle gamely to church, although totally reliant on his Zimmer walking-aid. He assured the vicar he would be quite all right as long as he could use his 'zither'.

From the parish magazine of Little Peover, Cheshire:
'Parishioners will be glad to know that the vicar is recovering well from his unpleasant disposition.'

A future cathedral dean, leading the Litany at an ecumenical gathering, prayed 'that it

may please Thee to eliminate all bishops, priests and deacons. . . .'

A parishioner in Co. Durham was reflecting on the irony that so many church buildings had become derelict despite the great wealth accruing to 'the Church Commissionaires'.

'It's as you say every Sunday, Father,' an elderly lady remarked to the Rev. Peter Miln. 'There's nothing but trouble in this transistory life.'

A bride-to-be, overcome by pre-nuptial strain, said she hoped there would be people outside the church, throwing 'spaghetti'.

A church organist in Chicago received a special request from a bride-to-be's mother for a piece of wedding music entitled, so far as she could remember, 'Jesus Walking Through Garfield Park'.

It turned out that she meant 'Jesu Joy of Man's Desiring', by Bach.

A church organist in Kent notified his Parochial Church Council that the 'Larigot' stop on the organ would have to be replaced. He had some trouble subsequently in persuading the PCC that what he needed was not a 'nanny goat'.

From the aviation world, I hear of a jet plane which disturbed a malapropist with its 'Masonic' bangs . . . and of a pilot, forced to leave his aircraft in a hurry by way of the 'ejaculation-seat'.

'Frightened? I was putrified . . .'

The malapropist on heat

'Well, of all the unmedicated gall . . .'

'Now I've really got my gander up . . .'

'You nincompimp!'

'It's enough to make your head stand on end . . .'

'I wouldn't touch him if he were a ten-foot Pole.'

'Ha! Hoist by your own leotard!'

'He's behaving like a complete cyclepath.'

'That's quite enough of your insinnuendoes.'

'Angry! I nearly blew my casket!'

'Well, that's really put the cap on the pigeon . . .'

'I'll have you know I'm not totally illiteral.'

'This smells to high herring . . .'

'We'll soon nip that idea in the butt.'

'What a load of bladderdash!'

'Frightened? I was putrified!'

'I really thought I'd given up the goat.'

The Clerk to the Justices in Newcastle-upon-Tyne reports that a witness in his court recently claimed to be in receipt of 'infidelity' benefit.

Divorce cases in British courts frequently turn on the question of 'congenial' rights, or whether a married couple have proved, as they claim, 'totally incombustible'. Petitioners in possession of decrees nisi have many times confirmed that, after six months, they wish their divorces to become 'obsolete'. There was also the co-respondent who, asked to describe his relationship with the defendant wife, assured the judge that it had been 'purely plutonic'.

While covering Cambridge Magistrates Court, I heard a policeman feelingly describe the distress of a woman to whose burgled house he had been called.

'How would you describe her condition when you arrived?' asked Prosecuting Counsel.

'She was in a collapsable state, sir,' the PC replied.

A passionate advocate of rescuing the Falkland Isles from Argentina declared that, after all, Falklanders were 'neuterised British subjects'.

His jingoistic soul was stirred to see the British Task Force sail out of Portsmouth, led by 'HMS Herpes'.

'Parlez-vous Francaise un peur?'

British xenophobia has always been best expressed in our attitude to the language of our nearest neighbours. For a thousand years, most Britons have refused to believe that French can mean anything at all unless transliterated to the nearest possible semblance of English. We say 'You can't make a silk purse out of a sow's ear' because our ancestors could not bring themselves to pronounce the French word 'souzière', meaning a cheap cloth scrip. And if the result should be pure gibberish — as when British soldiers in the Great War adapted the Frenchman's classic verbal shrug — well, San Ferry Ann.

The late Kenneth Tynan had an incurable weakness for making French turn phonetic handsprings into English. Tynan it was who rewrote the well-known nursery rhyme to begin 'Un petit d'un petit sat on a wall . . .' and invented the famous French strict tempo orchestra leader 'Charles-Louis d'Ince'.

The whole French attitude of isolationism, Tynan used to say, could be summed up in the pithy gallic maxim 'Pas d'elle yeux rhône que nous'.

51

Laura Corrigan, the famous Society malapropist of the 1930s, confided to James Lees-Milne how much she was enjoying a biography of 'Richard Gare de Lyon'.

A British ex-serviceman, winner of the Croix de Guerre for heroism, can sometimes be persuaded by his grandchildren to show them what, with typical modesty, he calls 'my Crossed Cigars'.

'Parlez-vous Francaise un peur? Vous comprenez? Good — then you're the missing link this dynamic young sales executive needs . . .'
Advertisement in Girl About Town

A friend's mother, speaking of their forthcoming night railway journey through France, volunteered to try to reserve a couple of 'courgettes'.

The Rev Peter Miln is also a noted chef and — thanks to his Belgian ancestry — a fluent French-speaker. At a banquet he attended recently, a Frenchwoman seated on his left began confiding details of the liver trouble to which, like many French people, she is a martyr. Most of the meal was occupied by her harrowing description of this 'crise de foie'.

Towards the end, the Englishwoman seated on Mr Miln's right murmured sympathetically, 'Poor Father — I expect you get awfully tired of hearing about other people's crises of faith.'

The French wife of a *Times* reader always refers to the paper's Portfolio game as 'Profiterole'.

A trendy young Londoner decided to give the family's new French au pair girl a treat by taking her to the weekend market at Camden Lock.

As they passed a stall selling various kinds of savoury pancake, the trendy young Londoner jocularly inquired, 'Do you feel like a crêpe?'

The au pair girl — who had been taught that upper class English people flatten their vowels, and who therefore thought she was being asked 'Do you feel like a crap?' — looked understandably confused.

Travel continues not to broaden the malapropist's mind. However our world may shrink, there will always — one hopes — be travellers in Greece changing their money into 'draculas'; in Spain and Italy visiting the many shrines to 'St Mary Mandolin'; in Switzerland admiring the picturesque alpine 'shillelaghs'; and in Hawaii photographing an authentic 'loo owl'.

I hear from visitors to Saudi Arabia that great kindness and hospitality is shown to

St Mary Mandolin

westerners by the region's 'bed-ridden' tribes-
men. And that in India, even more than
midland Britain, one sees Sikhs with 'turbines'
on their heads, and women attired in colourful
'safaris'.

Disturbing news comes from Alan Crompton
that his mother was swimming in the
Mediterranean when a jellyfish swam up and
wrapped its 'testicles' around her. Apparently,
holidaymakers are reluctant to visit South
America because of the 'toreadors' that have
lately caused such destruction there. More
and more people seem to be trying adventure
holidays in African countries where one can
still go to sleep listening to the sound of native

55

'tum-tums'. And I am pleased to hear that Bali seems every bit the island paradise it has been painted. A recently returned traveller reports that Balinese sunsets can contain 'all the colours of the rectum'.

Brian Rust, of Pinner, Middlesex, remembers his mother's firm belief that Albanians were people with white hair and pink eyes; that Red Indian war dances took place around a 'talcum' pole; and that, if our leaders did not take care, we might soon be at war with 'Solvent' Russia.

While staying at the Mandarin Hotel, Hong Kong, in 1974, I realised that the next day was my mother's birthday. I telephoned down to the front desk and dictated a greetings telegram, hoping it would reach her Bayswater flat in time.

That evening, a copy of the telegram had been pushed under my door. At the bottom, to my consternation, I saw the word 'Col.'* Surely I had not succumbed to journalistic reflex and sent the message collect. Fearful that my mother might have had to pay for her own telegram from the other side of the world, I telephoned the front desk again. The same Chinese voice as before answered me.

'This is Mr Norman. You sent a telegram to England for me today.'

'Yes.'

56   *in cable-ese, collate — ie, supply copy.

'I want to check something — it wasn't collect, was it?'

'Yes, sir,' the desk-clerk replied indignantly. 'It was *quite* collect!'

During the sixties, a delegation from the British shipbuilding industry paid a visit to several large shipyards in Japan.

'What do you find is your biggest problem?' one delegate asked his Japanese counterpart.

'Our biggest probrem,' the Japanese shipbuilder replied, 'is lust.'

The statement was greeted with sympathetic British nods.

57

A recent visitor to West Germany was clearly affected by that country's strident musical heritage as he described the delay he had experienced while changing trains in Bonn.

'I was stuck for hours,' he lamented. 'All the departure boards were empty and there wasn't a single announcement over the Tannhäuser.'

The incorrigible Laura Corrigan, disembarking from the yacht on which she had been cruising, said it felt wonderful to be on 'terracotta' again.

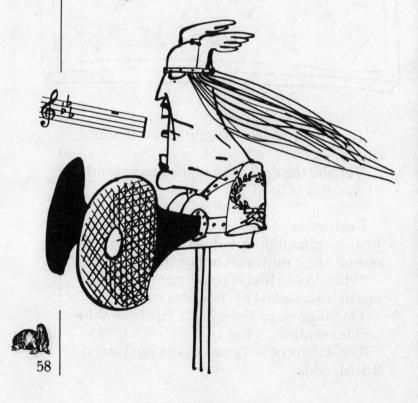

A traveller just back from Italy has been telling friends how awe-struck she was on first seeing the Leaning Tower of Pizza.

Richard Burton was once buttonholed in an hotel lobby by an American who claimed intimacy on the strength of also having Welsh forebears.

'You and I ought to get on well, Mr Burton,' he said. 'We're both Selts.'

'No,' Burton replied. 'I am a Selt. *You* are a sunt.'

Tommy Dorsey, the Big Band era's most famous malapropist, once introduced a guest vocalist — of coincidental beefiness — as 'that talented singing steer'. Among Bluesmen, Big Bill Broonzy was noted for his inability to remember any fellow Bluesman's name: he would refer to Scrapper Blackwell as 'Black Scrapwell' and to Fats Waller as 'Fat Wallace'.

All the poignant wisdom of the Blues seems gathered into a remark made by pianist Eubie Blake a few days before his 100th birthday.

'If I'd known I was going to live so long,' he said, 'I'd have taken more care of myself.'*

*He died three days later

A British Rail guard on the Waterloo-Portsmouth service explained over the internal loudspeaker system that the train would be delayed 'owing to a fertility on the line'.

Interesting dogs are owned by malapropists. They include the Cockerel Spanner, the Irish Settler, the Great Dame, the sausage-shaped Datsun and the small — but always game and playful — Shitzy-Witzy.

The Great Dame and the Shitzy-Witzy

'Every morning, he gets this terrible insurrection . . .'

The choicest malapropisms tend to be seasoned with Vim and wax polish and the smell of milk coming to the boil for mid-morning coffee. It is no more than fair to devote a full chapter to the inexhaustible verbal treasury of the British cleaning lady.

'He asked me to marry him twice, but I infused him.'

'I knew it was my coat because it had my entrails in it . . .'

'He drives the motorbike and she sits on the pavilion.'

'I've always been thin. When I was a girl, I was in bed for a year with infantile paraphenalia.'

'I hate injections. That's why I couldn't be a blood doughnut.'

'He's given her a gold singlet ring . . .'

'I couldn't eat any more. I was full to captivity.'

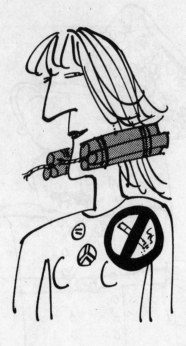

'*My daughter's bought a lovely new pair of dynamite earrings.*'

'*She's on this terrible diet — she's getting really emancipated.*'

'*He wore his uniform for a long time after the War. You see, he couldn't afford a new set of privvies.*'

'*She asked me if I liked the new colour scheme in her kitchen. I said "I'm not enamelled of it . . ."*'

'*She's changed her name you know. She done it by Interpol.*'

'*These Russians are always defecating, aren't they?*'

'*— he was walking round, starch naked.*'

'*Beautiful skin she's got. Just like allyblaster.*'

M. Richards, of London SW1, had ordered a wine rack from the Army and Navy Stores. A note from his cleaning lady said: 'The Army and Navy phoned. Your wild rat has arrived.'

C. C. Lindsay, of Croydon, remembers an arch-practitioner named Mercy, who announced she was giving her nephew a 'manicure set' for his birthday. Closer investigation revealed that she meant a Meccano set.

Employing a rare anagrammatic talent, Mercy said she knew a certain neighbour was back from holiday, having seen her in 'the telephone eskimo'.

For some years, Agnes Rodgers of Melton Mowbray organised an annual 'Alfresco Fete', which her cleaning lady always referred to as 'Your frisky feetie'.

The cleaning lady came in one day to report that her daughter had been taken to the opera by a highbrow boyfriend.

'Which opera?' Mrs Rodgers asked.

'Hyena,' the cleaning lady replied.

'I gave her her train fare,' a Stafford cleaning lady reported about her granddaughter's journey south. 'I didn't want her highjacking her way up and down that motorway.'

A South London cleaning lady was confiding in her employer about the 'demands' still made on her by her 70-year-old husband.

'Every morning when he wakes up,' she said, 'he's always got this terrible insurrection.'

'It's a doggy dog world . . .'

Gems of malapropist philosophy

'A woman's place is in a home'

'No man is in Ireland'

'It's a doggy dog world'*

'We pass like chips in the night'

'I'd say it was a vicious circus'

'Never give up. Keep looking for the bluebeard'

'All that's just a splash in the pan'

'Life isn't all beer and kittens'

'I'll just chuck it up to experience'

*Dog eat dog

During his recent Thames Television series, London hairdresser Trevor Sorbie demonstrated a spiky new cut on a girl model of already advanced punkishness.

As he began snipping, he explained that the idea was to make the final look 'as deranged as possible'.

During the 1983 Libyan Embassy siege, a local office worker told a colleague it would be impossible to get to work because police were throwing 'an accordion' around St James's Square.

While working as a probation officer in Derby, Eric Wall encountered a young

delinquent's parents who admitted they were not married, but said they had been 'happily co-rabbiting for years'.

A friend of actor and Soho-dweller Richard Huggett was enthusing about the recent great improvement in Leicester Square.

'It's so much better,' he said, 'now that it's become a pederastrian precinct.'

Prawns in the Game

Brian London, that lachrymose British heavy-weight, summed up the predicament of many a modern sports personality when he gazed at his interviewer, as emotionally as a British heavyweight could gaze, and remarked, 'I'm just a prawn in the game.' Pinioned by TV lights, chivvied by microphones to explain the inexplicable — generally at moments of high physical stress — who among us would not tumble into the same communal bath of gibberish? It is as unfair to mock sports commentators for howlers committed under the strain of perpetual improvisation. It is quite unfair: still, we shall go ahead with it.

When Beau Jack, the American fighter, fell on hard times, he would beg his former promoters to give him any match, even without prize money, 'just to relieve the monopoly'.

Ivor Powell, the Welsh manager of Port Vale F.C., used to attribute his team's good results to 'the harmonium in the dressing-room'. At moments of mid-match excitement,

he was heard to shout at his forwards: 'I've told you lads a hundred times! Veer *straight*!'

Commentating on the pursuit cycling event at the 1976 Montreal Olympics, the BBC's David Sanders observed: 'The East Germans are knitting well.'

Asked to comment on a disastrous game for his Philadelphia Phillies football team, coach Danny Ozark replied, 'Even Napoleon had his Watergate.'

A sports news reader on Radio Luxembourg recently referred to 'former Olympic swimming star Dunce Goodhew'.

Jimmy Hill, the BBC's egregious football presenter, is fond of saying he has just been 'incommunicado' with this or that match correspondent over the studio telephone.

Alan Weeks, the athletics commentator, has been heard to enthuse about 'Marie Scott from Fleetwood, the 17-year-old who's really plummeted to the top . . .'

Ex-racing champion Jackie Stewart remarked of a certain Grand Prix: 'There's enough Ferraris there to eat a plate of spaghetti.'

Ken Barrington, the former England batsman, carried the art of malapropism from the crease into management. 'Pitch it up more,'

he once instructed a bowler when coaching the England Test team. 'You've got to catch the batsman in two man's land . . .'

Describing his own black, bushy hair, Barrington once said it was 'like a grenadier's fuzzby'. He would also recall that, though some of his early Test tours had been 'quite inoculous', others had been organised as badly as 'Gymkhana's [Fred Karno's] Army'.

His most dramatic story was of witnessing a riot in Bangalore when, he said, the police 'infiltrated the crowd with a couple of hundred plain clothes protectives.'

Commentating from Israel, the BBC's David Vine observed: 'Today, the Holy Land is a Mecca for tourists . . .'

'Once again, it was the swimming pool that set the crowd alight.'

Radio 2 Olympic report, 1980

'In a moment, we hope to see the pole vault over the Satellite . . .'

David Coleman at the Montreal Olympics

'Now Juantareno opens his legs — and really shows his class. . . .'

Ditto

On television last season, American football coach Bill Peterson, admitted that a disappointing game by his team, the Houston Oilers, had left him 'utterly chestfallen'.

However, he thought he had found the 'crutch' of the problem and from here on would be trying an entirely new 'floormat'.

He added that the Oilers were being urged to dismiss every thought from their minds save that of reaching the Superbowl championship.

'I'm telling them, "Night and day, you guys should be thinking just one thing . . . *Sugar bowl*!"'

A recent TV documentary about vandalism focused on the plight of an old man living alone and neglected in one room in one of the worst affected areas. The old man was, however, tough, self-reliant and devoid of self-pity. He could stand his poor conditions, he told his interviewer — what depressed him were 'the evangelists who come round at night, smashing windows and kicking in the doors.'

Miss A. Chapman, of Forest Gate, London, tells me how fond her mother used to be of that fine English oratorio 'The Dream of Geronimo'.

John Parker remembers how impressed one of his most distinguished York University colleagues was by the first volume of Lord

Clark's autobiography — in particular, the chapters dealing with Clark's Edwardian idle-rich father.

'He never did a day's work after he was twenty,' Mr Parker's colleague reported. 'He bought a whole series of yachts, owned an hotel in France — he even broke the bank at Monte Cassino.'

An elderly aunt of Peter Ustinov came from Russia to Britain during the crisis days of World War II. Travelling by train during the blackout, she was perplexed to find all the station name-boards obliterated. Time and again, as her train flashed through, the only word that could be distinguished on a darkened platform was the ghostly legend 'Gentlemen'.

Arriving at her destination, the short-sighted old lady asked why so many different places in Britain were all called 'Cheltenham'.

'You can't have your pound of flesh and eat it too . . .'

Malapropists in the Media

The crimes against language perpetrated daily by newspapers, radio and television seldom include anything so harmless and amusing as a malapropism. Witless clichés, inane mixed metaphors and other consequences of striving for effect without thought, in general leave us as insensible to the words as are their users. We should be all the more grateful for these occasional blunders into vividness.

'Astronaut Alan Shepard is just beginning the final run through of his chick-list . . .'
ABC-TV commentary, Apollo Moon landing, 1972

'Tonight's orchestral concert comes to you from the Bath Room at Pump . . .'
BBC Third Programme, 1950s

'A new film by Jacques Cousteau, the famous French underwear explorer . . .'
Channel 13 TV, New York

William Deedes, editor of the *Daily Telegraph,*

Jacques Cousteau, the French underwear explorer

is cherished by Fleet Street, not only for his way of pronouncing 'shome mishtake', but also for what his staff called Deedesisms — a mixture of malapropism and mixed metaphor brought on by the great man's besetting vagueness. When a *Telegraph* reporter left the paper to join a magazine, Deedes shook his hand warmly and said, 'Goodbye my dear chap. Remember — don't burn your boots.'

Deedesisms can enliven the *Telegraph*'s political line, as when the editor remarked to a leader-writer, 'That Peter Carrington, you know, still weighs a lot of ice . . .' On the trials of editorship, Deedes has been heard to observe variously that 'You've got to keep all your feathers in the air', 'You can't make an omelette without frying eggs' and, most runically, 'You can't have your pound of flesh and eat it too.'

'Don't go away, folks. After the break, we'll have a wildlife expert here, and he's going to show us a horny owl . . .'
Johnny Carson on The Johnny Carson Show

The *County Express*, Stourbridge, recently reported a talk on smocking and rugs at Wordsley Community Centre as 'a talk on smoking drugs'.

During World War II, the exiled King Carol of Romania agreed to broadcast over the BBC from London to sustain the morale of his subjects under Nazi rule.

The poignant drama of the occasion was somewhat spoiled by the unsuitably merry sound which broke out on the air immediately before the king began to speak. The BBC Sound-Effects department had been asked to provide a fanfare. But the sound-effects man's cue had been accidentally mistyped as 'funfair'.

Some novel musical celebrities currently being mentioned by radio disc jockeys in Britain and America:

John Lemon
Mick Jaeger
Daisy Doris
Cher Porno
*Elephants Gerald**
Gladys Knight and the Pimps

A commentator on American public radio recently cast his listeners' minds back to the 1972 'Watergate bake-in' and went on to recall how former President Richard Nixon had escaped impeachment by 'a hare's breath'.

Wedding reports in local newspapers are usually written with the aid of forms filled up by the couples themselves, or their parents.

*Ella Fitzgerald

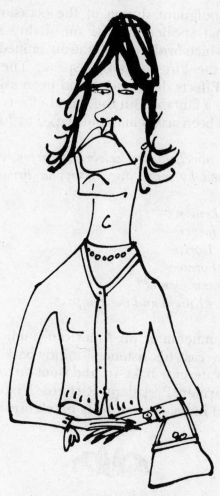

Mick Jaeger

As a junior reporter on the *Hunts Post*, I transcribed many accounts of services in which brides went to the altar carrying 'bunches of Friesians', and organists very often played that well-loved nuptial hymn 'Love's Divine'. A

certain bridal going-away outfit I shall always remember was detailed on the form as 'a lemon two-piece with a stone hat and matching accessories'. There was also the wedding gift of an elderly bridegroom to his rather

younger bride which a misplaced comma rendered, no doubt all too accurately, as 'an antique, pendant'.

An evening paper in the Midlands, some years ago, had to report the remarriage of its own managing director on the same Saturday as the start of the football season and the consequent reappearance, that same evening, of the football results edition popularly called The Sporting Pink, or Pink 'Un.

In the centre of the front page, the managing director was pictured with his mature bride outside the city Register Office. Next to their photograph appeared the jubilant announcement:

HURRAH! HURRAH! HURRAH!
The Pink 'Un Comes Out Again Tonight

A statement was issued last night by the British Broadcorping Castration . . .'
BBC Home Service, 1950s

The old-fashioned American police reporter was hired for his toughness and his ability to get on with both cops and hoodlums rather than his education or the elegance of his prose. Walter Head, of the old New York *Herald-Tribune*, recalls one such correspondent on the phone from the scene of a crime to his rewrite man, dictating:

'The cop fired. The bullet whickershammed off the wall and struck the corpse in the cadaver . . .'

Mr Head writes to me also of a suicide case when the police would allow only one reporter of the dozen-odd present to view the death scene.

As the nominee came downstairs again, his colleagues gathered round to hear the grisly details.

'Gentlemen,' he began impressively, 'the corp was dressed in . . .'

'You mean corpse don't you, John?' someone interrupted.

'There was only one for Chrissake,' John replied impatiently.

A Norfolk weekly paper published a fulsome obituary tribute to a woman famous for the flower arrangements she had provided at all the district's major social occasions.

'It will not be the same winter season without Mrs —,' the obituary said, 'and some of the most important balls in the county are going to miss her special touch.'

'At 8.50 tonight, we shall be broadcasting Haydn's Cremation . . .'

BBC Radio 3

Johnny Carson: 'We have Jack Nicholson on the show later.'

Charo (exotic Latin actress): 'Oh, I just love his movies.'

Carson: 'Did you see the one about the sanitarium?'

Charo: 'Oh yes — One Flew Over the Cuckoo's Nuts . . .'

Ray Seaton, of Wombourne, Staffs, reminds me of the colourful mistakes sometimes make by typists who take down journalists' copy over the telephone. As a reporter on the old Leicester *Evening Mail*, he once 'phoned in' the report of a public meeting where reference had been made to Pandit Nehru. It was taken down by the copytypist and printed as 'Bandit Nehru'.

A news bulletin in French on the BBC World Service included an item about population levels in the Cape region of South Africa. Impelled by Spooner's ghost, the announcer

referred at one point to 'La copulation immense du Pape'.

The source of most inadvertent filth in newspapers was the tendency of the old Linotype machine to substitute the letter i for o or a. Thus many a famous footballer was said to have 'sent a magnificent long shit over the bar'. Thus *The Times*'s famous reference to Queen Victoria's opening of the Forth Bridge, when it stated that 'The Queen herself graciously pissed over the magnificent edifice.'

The worst such substitution I ever knew — a rogue example — happened on the *Hunts Post* in a story I had written about a female youth leader's visit to Huntingdon on an exchange scheme, and the official lunch which had marked her departure.

The copy I wrote said 'At the conclusion of the lunch, Molly thanked all the Borough Councillors who had taken part in the scheme.' It appeared in the *Hunts Post* as 'At the conclusion of the lunch, Molly whanked all the Borough Councillors who had taken part in the scheme.'

'*The girl has been flown to America for treatment of a spinal tuna . . .*'

BBC Radio 4 News

At the end of the sixties there was a staff purge on one of the leading Sunday colour supplements. Among the casualties was an executive who had previously dominated the

magazine with grittily sentimental stories about working class life in his native Tyneside. The new editor was an old Etonian with a classical education and no empathy whatever with pit heaps or whippets.

Over a pub lunch during the transition, the Tynesider spoke wistfully about an issue of the magazine he had always dreamed of organising — a 'theme' issue that would have summed up his whole view of journalism in the modern world. The pub was noisy, and it seemed to the new editor that his companion was repeatedly stating a portentous, though obscure Latin axiom: 'Non Sequiris Vox'.

He was in fact observing — as his journalistic masterpiece would have been headlined — 'There's none so queer as folks'.

From the commercial and clerical world, I hear of a company whose personnel manager is currently offering new employees substantial 'French benefits' . . . of a factory owner humanely trying to reduce staff by a process of 'nutrition' . . . of economic calculations being made for the next 'physical' year, and current correspondence kept in a 'pretending' file . . . of a particularly reliable clerical worker whose office manager told her not to consult him on every small matter, but wherever possible to use her own 'discrepancy'.

The richest clerical malapropisms tend to occur when Pitman's shorthand — a system of phonetic symbols — has to be transcribed by someone unwilling to perform the additional job of thinking. Hence, in a Hereford solicitor's office, the term 'res judicata' could be rendered by an indifferent typist from her shorthand as 'raise Judy Carter'. Hence, a half-witted temp doing invoices in an Oxford office could convert 'sum accrued due' unflinchingly into 'some crude Jew'. Hence, the unconscious pragmatism of a temp in a City of London merchant bank when she transcribed the dry words 'triennial balance-sheet' into the far more sporting 'try any old balance-sheet'.

Efficiency is, of course, not always accompanied by verbal alertness. A highly efficient PA, seeing that the boardroom tape recorder was malfunctioning just before an important directors' meeting, gallantly took down the complex proceedings in shorthand. Arriving late for lunch with a colleague, she explained she had been delayed by doing 'a hand job' for the directors.

'It's your name we're paying for, Mr Bloomfield . . .'

Demonstrating that malapropists are generally as deaf to names as to words — and that few *faux pas* are more galling to the recipient — we reprise our international cast of Goldwyn, Lennon, Kendall et al.

Leo Abse MP was being introduced to a meeting in his Welsh constituency by a chairman who, time and again, referred to him as 'Mr Abbs'.

Unable to stand it any longer, the MP leaned forward, twitched the speaker's coat-tail and whispered:

'Call me Abs-*ey*.'

'All right,' the gratified chairman whispered back. 'And you can call me Jonesey.'

In the 1930s, Samuel Goldwyn paid a huge sum to lure the best-selling novelist Louis Bromfield on to his payroll as a scriptwriter at MGM. Bromfield was assigned an office and a secretary — and then forgotten. Six months after arriving, he still had not been given a picture to write.

At length he went to Goldwyn and said his conscience would not allow him to accept so much money for doing nothing.

Goldwyn got up from his desk and slipped an arm kindly round Bromfield's shoulders.

'You don't understand,' he said. 'It's your name we're paying for, Mr Bloomfield.'

The architect Sir Edward Maufe arrived late for a formal banquet, but tried to make his entrance as discreet as possible. Approaching the president of the top table, he murmured, 'I'm Maufe.'

'But my dear chap,' the president demurred, 'you've only just got here.'

A secretary at Corgi Books recently put through a call from Jonathan Cape executive Ahna Stamatiou, informing her boss 'It's our Mr Matthews . . .'

While playing for George VI and his family at Windsor Castle in the 1940s, Louis Armstrong dedicated a number to the King with the words: 'Dis next one's for you, Rex.'

The American pop journalist Tony Scaduto, in his book about Mick Jagger's trial and imprisonment for drug possession in 1967, referred to the then editor of *The Times* as 'William Rees-Moog'.

When John Lennon met Harold Wilson in 1964, it was in the star-struck Wilson's capacity

as 'honorary barker' of the Variety Club of Great Britain.

Lennon, being violently hung over, was even more fuzzy about names than usual. Hearing Mr Wilson described as a barker — and remembering Britain's famous butterscotch manufacturer — he addressed the future prime minister throughout the function as 'Mr Dobson'.

During the days of cinema newsreels, one member of each camera crew was responsible for filling out the 'dope sheet' with information to be written into the commentary.

In the Ascot Royal enclosure, a 'dope sheet' man from Gaumont-British News approached a Society beauty whose hat had just been filmed — the Hon Mrs Watt-Piper.

'Can I have your name, please Ma'am?' he said.

'Watt-Piper,' the Society beauty replied, smiling brightly.

'None of 'em,' the man retorted with loyal pride. 'I work for Gaumont-British News.'

The Detroit radio commentator Hal Youngblood tells a feeling tale of going to interview Sir Clifford Curzon about the latter's forthcoming piano recital with the Detroit Symphony Orchestra. In the course of an hour, Youngblood found himself being variously addressed by Sir Clifford as 'Mr

Redpath,' 'Mr Wheelwright', 'Mr Greengrocer', 'Mr Goodpasture', and 'Mr Blackpool'.

At last, the interviewer gently pointed out that his name was, in fact, Hal Youngblood.

'Ah yes, of course. Forgive me,' Sir Clifford replied. 'When you get to my age, the memory's the first thing to go, Mr Shuttle-thwaite . . .'

Bidding farewell to Sir Samuel Hoare, after the British Foreign Secretary had visited MGM, Samuel Goldwyn added: 'Please give my best wishes to Lady W.'

Chrissie Kendall, the National Theatre's budding young Mrs Malaprop, has been heard to express deep admiration for the acting skill of 'Joan Playwright'. Ms Kendall's own agility at doing back-somersaults has sometimes led her to compare herself with 'Tallulah Hand-bag' (or even 'Tallulah Bunkbed').

While at drama school, she was advised to read Stanislavsky. She asked her friend Annette how the name was spelt.

'S.T.A.N. . .' Annette began.

'Oh, I know how to spell his *first* name,' Ms Kendall said with dignity.

The Swedish explorer Thor Heyerdahl had been filming late at BBC Television Centre and was waiting in the main lobby for a radio cab. After long delay, a cab drew up outside. The driver walked in, looked round, ignored

Thor Heyerdahl and sat down on a bench.

'Excuse me,' the explorer ventured. 'I think I'm the one you're waiting for.'

'Not me, mate,' the driver said. 'I was told to come and pick up four Airedales.'